Kiev▲

Caucasus

GEORGIA   ●Bolnisi

ARMENIA

Ani▲ ●Echmiadzin
(Vagarshapat)

Trebizond▲

Manzikert●

BLACK SEA

Lake Van

Aghtamar▲

R. Tigris

Patleina●

▲Tirnovo

MESOPOTAMIA

▲Ravanica

R. Morava

canica

Caesarea●

R. Euphrates

udenica
vo ●
Sopocani▲

●Boiana

Constantinople▲

CAPPADOCIA

Goreme
valley●

Qalat-Siman▲

●Aleppo

R'safah●   Dura-Europos▲

▲Zemen

MARMARA IS.

▲Nicaea

Decani●

Philippi●

Qalb Louzeh●

Ruweha●

Prizren●   ▲Nerezi

Binbirkilisse●

Taurus Mts.

Qasr-ibn-Warden●

Seleucia
Pieria●

Apamea●   ●Palmyra

Ochrid●

▲Salonika

MACEDONIA

Mount
Athos

CILICIA

Antioch (Kaoussie)

●Emese

Chios●   ●Ephesus

EPIRUS PHOCIS

ssano

Hosios Lukas▲ ▲Daphni

Corinth●   Athens●

PELOPONNESE

▲Mistra

CYPRUS

Lake Tiberias

Bosra●

Jerash●

Caesarea●

PALESTINE

Jerusalem●

Mount Nebo

Bethlehem●

CRETE

na

MEDITERRANEAN SEA

Alexandria●

Wadi-
Natroun●

eptis Magna

FAIYUM

The Early Christian and Byzantine World

GREGORIUS SERMO DEI · ΑΓΙΟΣ ΑΝΑCΤΑCΙΟ · BASILIVS

THE EARLY CHRISTIAN AND BYZANTINE WORLD

JEAN LASSUS

Professor at the Sorbonne, Paris,
Institute of Art and Archaeology

PAUL HAMLYN · LONDON

General Editors

TREWIN COPPLESTONE   BERNARD S. MYERS
London   *New York*

PREHISTORIC AND PRIMITIVE MAN
Dr Andreas Lommel, Director of the Museum of Eth-
nology, Munich

THE ANCIENT WORLD
Professor Giovanni Garbini, Institute of Near Eastern
Studies, University of Rome

THE CLASSICAL WORLD
Dr Donald Strong, Assistant Keeper, Department of
Greek and Roman Antiquities, British Museum, London

THE EARLY CHRISTIAN AND BYZANTINE WORLD
Professor Jean Lassus, Sorbonne, Paris, Institute of Art
and Archaeology

THE WORLD OF ISLAM
Dr Ernst J. Grube, Curator, Islamic Department, Metropolitan Museum of Art, New York

THE ORIENTAL WORLD
Jeannine Auboyer, Chief Curator, Musée Guimet, Paris
Dr Roger Goepper, Director of the Museum of Far Eastern
Art, Cologne

THE MEDIEVAL WORLD
Peter Kidson, Conway Librarian, Courtauld Institute of
Art, London

MAN AND THE RENAISSANCE
Andrew Martindale, Senior Lecturer in the School of
Fine Arts, University of East Anglia

THE AGE OF BAROQUE
Michael Kitson, Senior Lecturer in the History of Art,
Courtauld Institute of Art, London

THE MODERN WORLD
Norbert Lynton, Head of the School of Art History and
General Studies, Chelsea School of Art, London

PUBLISHED BY
PAUL HAMLYN LIMITED · DRURY HOUSE ·
RUSSELL STREET · LONDON W.C.2
FIRST EDITION 1967
SECOND IMPRESSION 1967

© PAUL HAMLYN LIMITED, LONDON 1967

PRINTED IN THE NETHERLANDS BY JOH. ENSCHEDÉ EN ZONEN
GRAFISCHE INRICHTING N.V. · HAARLEM

Previous pages: 'The Fathers of the Church'.
Mosaic from the Cappella Palatina, Palermo.

List of Contents

Colour Plates

Gold Medallion of Justinian. 534–538. Formerly in the
Cabinet des Médailles, Paris.

Introduction

The numbers in the margins refer to the illustrations: heavy type for colour plates, italics for black and white illustrations.

Works of art may be classified in various ways. They may be grouped according to their country of origin, as in 'Egyptian Art', according to period, which may take the name of one man, as in 'The Age of Augustus', or according to style, as in 'Gothic Art'. It is also possible, and just as legitimate, to study together all the works that have been inspired by the same religion.

It is obviously this last method that lies behind a work on Christian art. So, at the start, we should stop to consider the astonishing way in which this art flourished. Because twelve workers from Palestine travelled the world, the world was changed, spiritually changed, since men found a new purpose in life, but outwardly changed as well. To this day villages are grouped round their church towers and cities around their cathedrals. And the greatest artists, whatever their philosophical outlook may be, almost always turn, at some time or another, to the creation of a work inspired by Christianity. The modest texts of the Gospels constantly give rise to new pictorial interpretations, the Apocalypse again illuminates the heavens, again the tortured body is nailed to the cross.

All this is inextricably linked with our own lives. But it had to begin somewhere: the first church had to be built, the first symbols created, and the first Bible illustrated. There was a first 'Virgin and Child', a first 'Crucifix'. The spread of evangelism, the forms of the hierarchy, the relations between Church and State, the development of theology, the rise of devotion to the saints or of monachism —every aspect of Christian history is depicted in its art. It is reflected not only in what might be called ecclesiastical art, which serves the immediate requirements of worship and enhances the glory of the church itself, but also in popular art, where one can trace the hold of faith on the lives and souls of the people. This book is an attempt to describe the process by which Christian art originated, developed and spread during its first thousand years.

Religious art is subject to all the usual limitations imposed upon artistic creation. The first limitation is financial: the architect and painter must work within a budget, whether small, as with the primitive communities, or large, as when a converted state overwhelms the bishops with its generosity. Then scope is limited: religious art is utilitarian. It is obvious that church architecture, which has to conform to the rules laid down by the liturgy, must take into account the numbers of those participating in the ceremonies. A Christian church is not a pagan temple. An effort of imagination is required that will work within the accepted forms, that will be aware of the different kinds of building, past and present, which have fulfilled similar needs, and which in any case will be rigorously controlled by the client, whether the donor or the head of the community. Christian building reflects the development of the Church: a desire for glory soon became apparent which, because of historical circumstances,

made Christian art a triumphal art parallel to that of Imperial Rome.

Painting similarly found new subjects. Events which marked the origins of the Church were depicted for the instruction and edification of the devout and the great mysteries of the faith were represented. The painter was obviously not given a free hand, but was submitted to other limitations than those of the text he had been asked to illustrate.

The use of a work of art, defined in the commissioning by the customer, is little more than a given subject matter, a point of departure. In Christian art, the demands of the clergy were obviously more rigorous. A concern for orthodoxy, particularly in the East, led to the notion of iconography; the representation of each subject was fixed once and for all and was considered valid only in this form.

There was a traditional way, which was almost obligatory, of representing the Adoration of the Magi or Christ's entry into Jerusalem, and the subject took on a theological value when it was the Baptism of Christ, the Transfiguration or the Descent into Hell—scenes that have trinitarian or eschatological implications. Again, the 'portraits' of Christ or of the Virgin—said to derive from St Luke, who is supposed to have been a painter—or even from miracles, the veil of Veronica or heaven-sent images, had a mystical reality which must not be overlooked. The images of saints were soon given the power that the relics had had; the painters gave life and immediacy to the intercessors both in everyday circumstances and in the spiritual life. Their portraits had a power over the faithful similar to that formerly exercised by the statues of gods. From the idol to the icon, art was not only a means of expressing supernatural power, but made it live among men. This sacred nature of Christian art and the respect accorded to it contributed to its splendour but prevented innovations.

Furthermore consciously or unconsciously, each artist followed what his master had taught him; he was not even free on a technical level, he bore the imprint of a school or the influence of some famous predecessor. He could seldom escape from the general movement that determined the traditions and methods of each period, each region, sometimes of each town. Yet even in the anonymity that almost completely cloaks the art of primitive Christianity, we can see the emergence of individual personalities who establish themselves through the originality, the purity and the splendour of their work.

It is tempting no doubt to regard Christian art, particularly in its earlier stages, as a collection of archaeological documents, which provide evidence concerning the content of the teaching, the form of the liturgy, the expansion of missionary activity and the everyday life of the Church. But we must go further and seek the individual personality of each work as it expresses the spiritual life of the artist and also his ideal of beauty.

The Awakening

'Render... unto Caesar the things which are Caesar's, and unto God the things that are God's.' When these perfectly reasonable words were first spoken they were quite revolutionary. The Emperor Augustus, who had been dead some years, had become the object of a cult that was growing throughout the Roman world. During his own reign, Augustus had deified Caesar, but had tried to keep popular adulation within manageable proportions. In Rome, former citizens of the Republic still had reservations; but in the East, Hellenistic traditions helped to perpetuate a politically effective confusion; and in Africa, the Berber King Juba II had shown his gratitude by building a temple to the friend to whom he owed his throne.

Christianity was to be born and to develop in a world in which religion, the Empire and patriotism were closely linked. Temples were built to 'Augustus and Rome'. Venus, Caesar's mother, was the goddess of the Julia *gens*, or family, and protected the dynasty accordingly. At different times and under different dynasties, other gods were called upon to fulfil this role—Apollo, for example, or Jupiter and Hercules, or even Heliogabalus the sun-god who was worshipped at Emese in Syria. It was at the heart of this imperial paganism, this State religion, this ceremonial expression of loyalty to the imperial throne that Christianity was to develop.

There is no need to emphasise the restrictions that surrounded it. A Roman city was the physical embodiment of a monolithic system. In Rome the Capitol dominated the Forum, and the Forum was surrounded by temples. On the public squares of every provincial town were temples and statues of the gods and deified emperors—idols. The theatre was still a Dionysiac ceremony; the games that took place in the amphitheatre had a propitiatory value. Every army officer was bound by oaths to the gods; every imperial or municipal official was a priest in some way or other. A Christian would have had to stand aside from the public life of his time.

Yet the Christian communities flourished because they offered a more satisfying expression of the need both for brotherhood and a spiritual life of hope than did the mystery religions that came from the East at the same period. Gradually and unobtrusively, these communities grew. At first, they were composed entirely of ordinary people—Jewish and Syrian tradesmen grouped together in certain districts of Greek or Roman cities and a few pagan neighbours who had been attracted by the novelty of their religious witness. Slaves and artisans seem to be the first to be drawn to the new religion, and women. Only later, and much more slowly, did conversions take place in the wealthier or more intellectual classes. So, at the beginning, there was scarcely enough money to create a Christian art.

1. **The Good Shepherd.** 4th century. Mosaic. Basilica Theodoriana, Aquileia, Italy. Symbolic motifs already traditional in the Christian Church are set into the geometrical mosaic which paves the entire basilica. The familiar stance of the figure of the Good Shepherd carrying his sheep and Pan-pipes is found in catacomb paintings and sarcophagi of the same period.

2. **The Apotheosis of the Emperor Antoninus and his wife Faustina.** 161–169 AD. Marble. Cortile della Pigna, Vatican, Rome. This relief is from the base of the column of Antoninus Pius. The imperial couple are carried skywards by a winged spirit, in the presence of the goddess Rome and a personification of the river Tiber. Dead emperors were deified, even during their lifetime they became the object of a cult; there was a temple of Antoninus and Faustina on the forum.

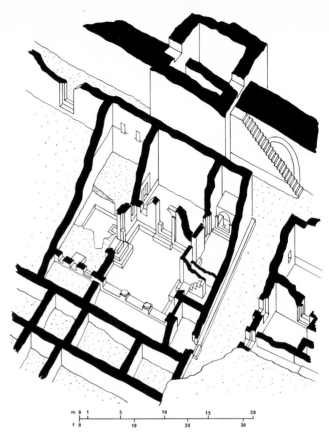

3. **Aerial view of Dura-Europos.** This fortified town, built in a loop of the Euphrates by one of Alexander's generals, has revealed in excavation precious evidence of the religious art of the Eastern world in the first centuries of our era. The town was captured and destroyed by the Parthians in 265, but a synagogue and a Christian church have been found, figure 4, plates 1, 2.

4. **Christian community house.** *c.* 230. Dura-Europos, Syria. The Christian community was housed in a dwelling which differed from all the others only in the baptistery (top right) where a large bath was installed under a canopy and the walls decorated with paintings recalling scenes of the Old and New Testaments.

Perhaps the need for such an art was barely felt, especially with the heritage of Jewish prejudices. When the communities began to include rich and influential citizens among their members the problem emerged of adapting the new faith to a world from which until then it had been kept apart. It was the duty of the clergy, the hierarchy that had now formed, to preserve the distinction between the Church and the world but in order to live each Christian had to accept compromises within it.

In a world in which art was official, imperial, and pagan, Christian art could only begin in a very small way. And, anyway, was it not in itself a compromise with the world? The pagan statues were for their worshippers the dwellings of the gods, while the Christians, in their turn, were convinced that they were inhabited by demons. How, therefore, should Christian statues be conceived? As images of the true God? The Jewish elements in the Church would abhor the idea. But there were other factors to consider. Prevented by poverty and then by prudence from erecting special buildings for their meetings—which, in any case, should never resemble temples—Christians met in houses that had been lent or given to the community by a rich convert. These houses would be altered a little—a few walls might be knocked down to provide a larger room. Very often the Hellenistic or Roman decoration of the house was left unchanged. In a period of expansion, and conversion, in Christian as in Mithraic practices, the initiation ceremony—here adult baptism—had obviously

to be given its full significance. On Easter night, in a specially arranged room, the catachumens were plunged three times in a decorated bath.

These early churches were so modest that for a long time archaeologists were unable to discover any of them. Sometimes they were destroyed by persecutions, particularly the last, that of Diocletian in 305. More often, after the triumph of Christianity, they were effaced by the increasingly ambitious buildings that replaced them—this is what happened to the parishes of ancient Rome—the 'titular churches'. The basilicas of the 11th, 13th and 18th centuries were built on the sites of the meeting-places that had been given to the community in the 3rd century by Equitius, Vizans or Aemiliana.

The identification as primitive churches of buildings of very varying form which have been excavated beneath later churches has given rise to controversy—as in the case of the Christian community house, called 'titulus Equitii', which certain scholars believe they have recognised beside the basilica of S. Martino ai Monti. Elsewhere, it seems that the rooms used by the communities for their meetings were situated on the first floor, above a row of shops, as at Sta Anastasia, or over large, dark warehouses, as at S. Clemente. Even if, as in the second case, a very large room had been opened out, the building had no distinctive appearance from the outside. Its nearest neighbour, on the other side of an alley, was a sanctuary of Mithras. At SS. Giovanni e Paolo the community owned the whole

5. Wall-painting from the baptistery at Dura-Europos.
3rd century. Paint on plaster. Syria. The restored paintings
from the walls of the baptistery depict scenes from the Old
and New Testaments. In the top register of the right wall are
the *Healing of the paralytic* and *Christ walking on the Sea of
Galilee*. Below are the *Three Maries at the sepulchre*.

building: in a room on the ground floor, paintings have
been found of the martyrdom—apocryphal, as it happens
—of two saints, while the church itself was on the first
floor. However vague these results may be, they show that
the early Roman churches were unobtrusive, set up in
quite simple households and were not noticeable among
the buildings of the capital and probably of any large town.

DURA-EUROPOS

3 It was in Dura-Europos, a small fortified town on the
banks of the Euphrates, that a Roman garrison was besieged by the Parthians in 265. The Romans, fearing for the
safety of a wall that the enemy was undermining, built a
high embankment of soil and rubble behind the ramparts,
thus overrunning the nearby houses, and preserving a
church of the 3rd century recently rediscovered.

Dura was built by one of the generals of Alexander the
Great and was full of temples. In them the gods of Greece
and Rome were worshipped, of course, but also those of
Mesopotamia, Iran and Syria, the gods of the caravans of
Palmyra and the camel-rider's gods of the Arabs. There
was a Jewish community and a splendid synagogue covered
1,2 with paintings, a sort of illustrated Bible, revealing the existence of a Jewish art and a Jewish iconography that were
nevertheless forbidden by the law. And, on one street
4 corner, there was a house exactly like the others with a
baffle-type door and a square courtyard. There was a
room that had been enlarged, where a small platform had

been built, a dining room, and, in the corner—the only
notable alteration—a baptistery, with a bath surmounted
by a canopy and a few fragments of frescoes. The priest
probably lived on the upper floor.

Painted on the walls of the baptistery, in a very simple
style, similar to that of the paintings in the temple of the
town, were Adam and Eve, the Good Shepherd, Christ 5
walking on the waters, David and Goliath and a procession
of women carrying candles moving towards a lighted sarcophagus. In the large room—which was used for the meetings of the community—a frieze belonging to the former
owner, decorated with Pan-pipes and theatrical masks, had
been left untouched.

We have no reason to believe that the Christian community at Dura was at this time particularly small, or
particularly poor and timid. On the contrary, it seems
more likely that it was a missionary church, in which the
community grew more from adult conversions than from
its own children. It is a strange stroke of chance that has
thus allowed us to enter one of those churches of Mesopotamia, related to the synagogues of the *diaspora*, and to see
the problems of the Christian community house and of its
decoration in a setting that, at that date, was as oriental as
possible. The art of Dura has revived our knowledge of
what has been called 'Parthian' art, which was probably
the Alexandrine art of Asia. One can recognise at first
glance the conventions and ideas that were to constitute
certain of the characteristics of Byzantine art—the use of
'frontality', the absence of relief and the spirituality of the
faces. From the beginning Christian art had origins outside the Mediterranean world as well as within it.

In the larger cities, the churches may have been set up
in more satisfactory conditions and decorated more richly.
But it is certain that the Christian community houses were
generally of this humble kind, probably the house of one
of the faithful, and indistinguishable from the others. As
there were different types of house throughout the Roman
world, so the churches had no consistent architectural
style of their own. Thus, at the beginning of the 4th century, the church at Qirkbizé, in northern Syria, with its 6
enclosed courtyard, its colonnade on the south side and all
the detail of its building, looked very like the fine house
next door to it—as it still does, despite the alterations of
subsequent centuries.

Perhaps there already existed a certain choice of themes
that were represented on the walls—and perhaps definite
ways of representing them. The very existence of decoration of such a rich and assured iconography in the synagogue at Dura leads one to believe that the primitive
Church had access to the same kind of model books that
resulted in pagan mosaic floors at the same time being
executed in a comparable form throughout the Roman
world. In any case, even if the paintings of the church in
Dura did belong to local art, they are not as exotic as
might be imagined, but are conceived in the same way as
the paintings in the Roman catacombs.

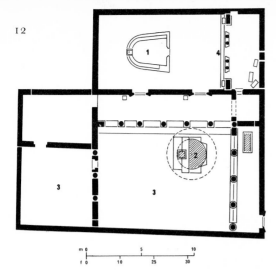

7. **The Christian cemetery.** 6th century. Timgad, Algeria.
A southern view of the cemetery which consisted of very
simple tombs made of large tiles sunk into the earth. They are
unembellished with funerary equipment.

8. **Catacomb of S. Panfilo, Rome.** 3rd or 4th century.
The narrow corridors were hollowed out of the rock bed, *loculi*
were carved in the walls of them thus permitting large numbers
of bodies to be buried in a piece of land of restricted
surface area.

6. **The church of Qirkbizé.** 4th century. Northern Syria.
The church is of a form very close to that of the neighbouring
house. The development of the liturgy in the 4th and 5th
centuries imposed certain modifications in its interior and
exterior arrangements—1, Bema, 2, the cistern, 3, courtyards,
4, iconostasis.

EARLY CHRISTIAN BURIAL

One of the fundamental articles of the Christian faith was
the belief in the Second Coming of Christ. The apocalypse
of John—among other apocalypses—had described in
advance the terrible day when the Lord would appear
from the clouds in all his glory and judge the living and the
dead. At the sound of the trumpet the dead would rise up.
The bodies would return to life and be joined to their souls
and men would be called to account for their sins. This
theme of the resurrection of the body, as seen in the story of
the prophet Ezekiel, had been depicted on the wall of the
synagogue at Dura. For the first Christians, this return of
Christ, victorious over death, was imminent—and even
after the beginning of the 2nd century, it was expected to
occur from one day to the next. In the end, they anticipated
that the prophecy would take place in an indefinite future,
but the hope of resurrection nevertheless remained central
to Christian thought.

This is probably why Christians were forbidden to
cremate the dead, a practice which alternates in human
history with burial and was, at this time, almost universally
accepted. The Romans used cremation; their ashes were
put into urns, and these urns were either buried or placed
in niches in the *columbaria*. There was a marked return in
the 2nd century to the practice of burial, perhaps under
the influence of Christianity. As a result, new problems
were created for the cemeteries. Space was needed, especially for the Christians, who insisted on preserving something of the individuality of their dead.

The Christian communities began to help families to
solve this problem. It was of course more difficult in the
case of the poor than of the rich—and most of the faithful
were poor. Moreover, they wished to be buried together,
among their brothers. So from the middle of the 2nd century Christian cemeteries were created. Usually these consisted of reserved areas in the open air outside the city walls, 7
where, as with pagan burial, the bodies were placed between two rows of tiles forming a roof. Above ground there
was an inscribed stele or a plain monument. Sometimes,
however, the bodies were placed in stone sarcophagi,
juxtaposed. Sometimes vaults were dug in hillsides or in
rock faces—where sarcophagi were often carved out of the
rock itself, often under arches, hence their name *arcosolia*. 3
It was particularly in Rome that Christians adopted a
form of cemetery that had previously but infrequently been
used by pagans: these consisted of a network of subterranean tunnels known as catacombs. Because it was important to make the best possible use of the land available the 8
tunnels were very narrow. Moreover when in one tunnel all
the *loculi* were full, the height and depth of it were increased
in order to add more. Then new tunnels would be dug out
at a lower level and further tunnels branched off it in different directions. All this resulted in those impressive labyrinths around Rome which are so extensive that new ones
are still being discovered.

At first, like the 'houses of the Christians', these cemeteries were on private land, which had been put at the disposal of the community by individual members. However, by the 3rd century it appears that the right of association recognised by the Romans enabled them to be regarded as Church property and to be maintained by the Church. This, of course, implies that the imperial administration and the police knew of both the churches and cemeteries and tolerated them, unless some special event —a local crisis or an imperial decision—set off a wave of persecution.

In these cemeteries the bodies of the martyrs were laid beside those of their fellow-Christians. At first both received visits, honours and gifts, as was the custom in Roman society. To these were soon added prayers for the repose of the dead and prayers to the martyrs requesting their intercession. But the catacombs were not intended to be places of worship, nor to be used as underground refuges for the persecuted. They played exactly the same role as the 'open-air' cemeteries in the provinces of the empire.

CATACOMB PAINTINGS

Funerary art is, in our day as well, essentially a matter of simple craftsmanship when it is created for families of modest means. It would be excessive to regard as great works of art the paintings with which the Christians **3,9** decorated the galleries and *cubicula* of the catacombs. They derive from that sketchy, but charming decorative art that, after Pompeii, was used in most Roman houses—and which could be adapted without effort to new subjects. This Christian decoration is strongly reminiscent of the paintings in private houses. Often, the traditional motifs —cupids, the seasons, animals—are intermingled with the themes created by the Christians.

These themes were very simple and, at first, purely **10a,b** symbolic—anchors, fish, baskets full of loaves, and vines with birds pecking at them. There was the Good Shep- **4,5** herd, borrowed from the pagan art of the time, and represented sometimes as a shepherd, surrounded by his flock and playing on a bucolic pipe, and sometimes carrying a sheep on his shoulders. There is the *orans*, the figure **6,9** of the woman praying, with her arms raised, who represents the soul of the dead person—whether a man or a woman— rather than an actual dead woman. This theme is treated either as a symbolic motif or, on the contrary, as a figure surrounded with flowers representing the gardens of Paradise. If we recall the Shepherd of Hermas and the visions of St Perpetua, both these pastoral and floral scenes may be seen as visions of the place of light and peace.

A certain number of scenes taken from the Old and New **8** Testaments are also to be found on the walls of the catacombs, but they are treated in so schematic and elementary way that only the faithful could recognise the subject. They suggest rather than represent, and were not a method of pictorial instruction for those who could not read the Bible as later Christian frescoes were to be. Prior knowledge is needed to recognise the man cured of the palsy in

9. **Evocation of Paradise.** Wall-painting from the catacomb of Callixtus, (after Rossi). The decoration of the catacombs stresses the salvation of souls which is evoked by symbols, or by sketchily drawn scenes.

10a, b. **The miracle of the loaves and fishes.** (a) Painting from the crypt of Lucina, Catacomb of Callixtus, Rome. (b) Pavement mosaic from et-Tagbah (Heptapegon), Israel, in the Church of the Multiplication of the Loaves and Fishes. Mid-5th century. The representation is almost the same in Rome as the one in the place where the miracle occurred.

11. **Sarcophagus of Adelphia.** 4th century. Marble. Syracuse. The two registers of the sarcophagus are broken by a shell with busts of the deceased. On the cover can be distinguished scenes from the life of the Virgin, then to the right the shepherds at the crib. In the top register among other biblical scenes are *Christ foretelling Peter's denial*, and the *Healing of the woman with an issue of blood*; to the right *Moses receiving the law*, the

Sacrifice of Abraham, the *Healing of the blind man*, the *Multiplication of the loaves and fishes* and the *Raising of the widow's son from the dead*. Below: *The young Hebrews before Nebuchadnezzar*, the *Miracle at Cana*, the *Adoration of the Magi*, *Adam and Eve* and the *Entry into Jerusalem*. It is a good example of the complex iconography of the early sarcophagi.

the figure of a man carrying his bed upon his back; or

11 Noah in another figure whose bust emerges from a four-legged coffer (*arca*, in Latin) and whose hand reaches out

10 to hold a bird; or Jonah in the handsome young man asleep under a trailing gourd; Daniel in the lion's den looks more like an ancient Gilgamesh—an *orans* standing between two crouching animals. And the feeding of the five thousand, a prefiguration of the Eucharist, is sym-

10a, b bolised by a basket filled with loaves and fishes. It has often been thought that the choice of such methods of representation was a result of the enforcement of secrecy. But even when the scene represented involves several figures, decorative elements and exotic costumes, they are not necessarily any more explicit for the uninitiated. Three

9 young men standing in the middle of flames, full face and with their arms outstretched, what could this signify to someone who did not know of the punishment inflicted by Nebuchadnezzar on three young Hebrew blasphemers? And how can the man striking a rock with a stick and causing a spring to flow be recognised as Moses, if one does not know that Moses miraculously gave drink to his people in this way. More elaborate images appear later, the adoration of the Magi, for example, or banqueting scenes, representing perhaps a funeral ceremony, the eucharistic

9 meal or an episode in the heavenly life of the blessed.

The range of subjects is limited, but there are a great many repetitions and variations. This is not from a lack of imagination, but out of choice. The scenes of Paradise provide a clue to the explanation of other subjects. These **12** are the promises that the dead take with them into the next life, where they must observe their realisation, because the miraculous aid that the god of the Old Testament so often gave his people and the help given by Christ to those he met as he travelled were guarantees of future salvation.

Representations of daily life also occur in the catacombs, as in pagan funerary art: there are scenes, for example, of masons building a house, tradesmen in their shops and, above all, grave-diggers, who found themselves at home in these labyrinths that they had dug.

The style of all these paintings is flowing and relaxed; the colours are bright and gay, and light touches were necessary if the paintings were to be seen by lamplight. The attitudes and movements of the figures are boldly conceived, the faces are usually only sketched in—except, sometimes, in the case of praying women, when they may have been portraits. These paintings are rarely framed, but are generally placed against a light background, or sometimes among more complex decorative compositions. These ancient works are rather more religious and his-

12. **Columnar sarcophagus.**
4th century. Marble. Lateran museum, Rome. The richly decorated columns separate the figures but give rythm and elegance to the composition. The scenes represented follow the traditional iconography; to the left is the *Sacrifice of Abraham*, followed by *Peter's arrest*, then in the centre *Christ triumphant hands the law to Peter*, and on the right the *Judgment of Pilate*. The lack of order in the scenes is typical of the sarcophagi.

13. **Symbolic sarcophagus.** 4th century. Marble. Lateran Museum, Rome. The entire front of the sarcophagus is covered with vine-trails peopled with *putti*, like some pagan Bacchic scene. Only the three statues of the Good Shepherd, standing on ornamental pedestals, indicate the transposition to Christian symbolism (see plate 6).

torical in import than properly artistic. The baptistery at Dura has shown that the houses of the Christians, like the subterranean cemeteries, were decorated with paintings based on similar themes and treated in the same spirit; consequently they may only be reflections. It would be unwise to judge primitive Christian art simply by the examples of it that have survived. It is possible that art of a quite different order flourished in the early churches, despite the restrictions imposed on them. Certain paintings discovered in Egypt, which are generally of a later period, may date nonetheless from before the *Pax Ecclesiae*. It may well be that archaeology has not yet said its final word.

EARLY CHRISTIAN SARCOPHAGI

The sarcophagus is a luxurious coffin—a long vessel hollowed out of stone, often marble, to fit the body which it protects and contains beneath a heavy monolithic lid. Sarcophagi can obviously be grouped together either in a subterranean tomb or in a built mausoleum, or simply placed on the ground in an open-air cemetery. They were often decorated, a custom the Romans—and the Christians in their turn—inherited from the Etruscans and the Greeks. A continuous development may be traced from the pagan sarcophagi of the 2nd century to the finest Christian coffins of the 4th. There is no break: the marble masons used the same tools, the same techniques and the same traditions. Only some motifs were new, and even then they sometimes kept the same subjects. There are Christian sarcophagi on which, as in the previous century, the seasons are represented by *putti*. There are lions mounting guard —not to mention the decorative background, the strigils, for example, or the colonnades. In the details of the figures and drapery, for instance, the tradition developed in exactly the same way as in official bas-reliefs. Occasionally, a mythological character or scene has been borrowed and incorporated in a Biblical scene; so Jonah lying under

the gourd has the appearance of the sleeping Endymion. The dead are still represented as busts in medallions.

So it is in the subjects, first of all, that Christianity expresses itself. The same motifs are to be found in sarcophagi as in the catacombs—particularly the use of symbolic figures, the Good Shepherd carrying the sheep on his shoulders and the *orans*. But they are blended with a traditional background of architecture or foliage.

The traditions of the workshops died hard, so that the Christian character of certain sarcophagi is dubious because of the difficulty in deciphering the symbolism of some of the motifs. But before long Biblical scenes are introduced and treated, as in the catacombs, in the most economic way. The most characteristic sarcophagi are like collections of pictures, sometimes juxtaposed and framed, sometimes even overlapping each other, so that the subjects can be recognised only by an experienced and attentive eye.

These subjects are curiously mixed. The Old Testament is well represented: Adam and Eve in the temptation scene, the sacrifice of Abraham, Jonah, the young Hebrews and Nebuchadnezzar, Moses receiving the Law, or striking water from the rock, Daniel among the lions, Job, and a great many others. The New Testament is represented first by the Gospel stories of Christ's childhood—the crib, the Magi—then by the miracles—the miracle of the loaves and fishes, the marriage-feast at Cana—and the miraculous cures—of the man born blind, of the man sick of the palsy, of the woman with an issue of blood, the raising of Lazarus and of the daughter of Jairus. Finally, there are the scenes of the Passion—the entry into Jerusalem, the Arrest, the judgement of Pilate, and sometimes, but in a symbolic form, the Crucifixion and the Resurrection. These pictures always seem to be assembled by chance, as if there was no logical or chronological link between the episodes. Their choice of scene has long been explained by

14. **Sarcophagus of the Empress Helena.** 4th century. Porphyry. 95 × 91¾ × 61 in. (225 × 233 × 155 cm.). Vatican Museum, Rome. Carved out of an enormous block of Egyptian porphyry the sarcophagus of St Helena, the mother of Constantine, was formerly in her tomb on the Via Appia. It is decorated with sculptures in high relief of Roman horsemen and barbarian prisoners. The motifs are treated separately probably because of the hard stone. The *putti* and garlands emphasise the purely triumphal character of the decoration.

the fact that they are a commentary on the prayers of the liturgy for the repose of the souls of the dead. They are references to the helping action of God—'protect him O Lord, as thou hast protected Daniel among the lions'. It is also possible that the texts, on which the scenes were based, were later forgotten by the sculptors who re-arranged the scenes according to their own needs—balancing their decorative band by putting the tomb of Lazarus on the left edge, for example, and Pilate's dais on the right.

In fact, amidst the pious intentions of these works, their artistic requirements are not lost sight of. Certain friezes possess an astonishing pictorial overcrowding such as was previously to be found on pagan sarcophagi; others are arranged in bands placed one on top of another—increasing the number of intercessions. A feeling for architectural form often makes its appearance: the friezes are then arranged on one or two storeys, like façades, and interspersed vertically with columns supporting architraves or arches. Some of these arrangements are highly successful —but these more beautiful sarcophagi usually date from the second half of the 4th century.

This period also sees the appearance of new subjects which are important enough in themselves to take up the whole decoration of a frieze. Such a subject might be a high-

ly graphic scene like the crossing of the Red Sea, treated in the same style as the victory of Constantine at the bridge of Milvius on his triumphal arch in Rome; or they might be compositions similar to those that were to be found in the apses of the basilicas—and which sometimes appear in the same period in the later catacomb paintings—such as Christ teaching the twelve apostles in a terrestrial scene or in paradise. 12

The richness, variety and fantasy of the Christian sarcophagi of Rome or Provence, for example, provide one of the most delightful aspects of primitive Christian art. Sometimes the execution is a little clumsy—it is, after all, the work of simple craftsmen—but the development of relief in this period must be taken into account. The short figures, with large heads full of movement and expression, are to be found not only on the sarcophagi but also on other bas-reliefs of the 4th century and in the painting of this period. The intention is one of dramatic evocation rather than pictorial composition. But these works do have great linear rhythm, the planes being divided up by columns or simply by the figure of Christ being endlessly repeated in the miracle scenes. He is taller than the other figures and has great presence and authority, which with the sobriety of his gestures, which never alter, is strongly reminiscent of the invocations of the funeral liturgy.

Before the *Pax Ecclesiae*, Christian funeral art was entirely the work of ordinary craftsmen; and as it was intended for private individuals, it did not undergo any dramatic change when the triumph of Christianity was finally confirmed. Paintings and sarcophagi followed an uninterrupted development, which explains the difficulties experienced by specialists when trying to pass from a relative chronology to an absolute chronology. There were developments in the style as well as in the choice of the subjects which would probably have occurred whether or not profound changes had taken place in the status of the Christian church of the 4th century.

The greatest effect on monumental Christian art was its link with the imperial State. It will be seen how 14 Christian art became not only free, but official. The bishops had formerly been poor and suspect: they could now request and obtain generous help from the Emperor. This resulted, of course, in a quite different and much richer art.

But however lacking the first communities had been in materials and money, often persecuted, and suspicious, too, of any kind of ostentation or of any tendency towards anthropomorphism, the works of their artists and craftsmen have retained their value—what might be called their sociological value, since they express as fully as the texts certain of the most original characteristics of the Christian communities; their spiritual value, since they represent an attempt to find an expression for the new faith, an incarnation in art of a religion of the spirit and of truth, and their artistic value, too, since the traditional forms were infused with a new spirit which affected even the hand of the sculptor and the painter.

1 (above). **West wall of the synagogue at Dura-Europos,** Northern Syria. First half of the 3rd century. Fresco transferred to Damascus Museum. The discovery of these paintings in the synagogue has revealed the existence of an Israelite iconography of the Bible. In the centre of the wall is the niche for the Book, surmounted by a painting of the Torah shrine, the Temple of Jerusalem and the seven-branched candlestick. To the right of this is the Elder's seat and around the walls the benches for the faithful. Among the biblical scenes are, below right, the *Anointing of David* and *Moses rescued from the waters of the Nile*. The last one clearly shows how the successive episodes in a story are incorporated in a single scene.

2 (left). Detail showing the Temple at Jerusalem, a prophet to the left, and above *Moses and the burning bush* and part of a scene depicting the *Crossing of the Red Sea*.

3 (opposite). **Cubiculum 'O'.** Mid-4th century. Paint on plaster. New Catacomb of the Via Latina, Rome. The overall effect of catacomb-painting in its more elaborate parts is clearly demonstrated in this view, with the individual motifs isolated against a plain background within a painted frame. Garlands, birds and geometrical decoration surround scenes from the Gospels and from everyday life. The niches to the right and left are the *loculi*, or graves, and in the *arcosolium* at the back is a sarcophagus beneath an arch hollowed out of the rock.

4 (above left). **The Good Shepherd.** Mid-3rd century. Paint on plaster. 31 in. (78 cm.) diameter. Ceiling of the Chamber of the Velatio, Catacomb of Priscilla, Rome. The theme of the Good Shepherd carrying a sheep is one of the most recurrent in Early Christian art.

5 (above right). **Pastoral scene.** 3rd century. Paint on plaster. 20 × 36 in. (50 × 91 cm.). Painting from the Catacomb of Domitilla, Rome. The Good Shepherd was often depicted surrounded by his flock in a pastoral scene, which might represent Paradise. Here he holds Pan-pipes, reminiscent of Orpheus, reflecting the way in which classical subjects were adapted by the Christians to their own meaning.

6. **Detail from a sarcophagus.** *c.* 270. Marble. Sta Maria Antiqua, Rome. The Good Shepherd carrying a sheep on his shoulders is depicted in the same way as in the catacomb painting. The trees form divisions between one subject and the next, and to the right can be seen part of the *Baptism of Christ*.

7. **Orans.** Late 3rd century. Paint on plaster. 27 × 80 in. (68 × 203 cm.). Painting in an *arcosolium* in the Coemeterium Maius, Rome, which depicts a woman with her arms raised in supplication and prayer. She stands in surroundings suggesting an earthly Paradise, flanked by two shepherds, one of them milking one of the flock, the other bringing a stray to the fold, under the watchful eyes of a dog. Beneath the painting are the *loculi* or graves roughly hewn out of the rock wall.

8 (left). **The Raising of Lazarus.** Late 3rd century. Paint on plaster. 32 × 44 in. (*c.* 81 × 111 cm.). Painting from the Catacomb of St Peter and St Marcellinus, chamber XIII, Rome. The extreme simplification of the Gospel scene, with Lazarus swathed like a mummy, prevented interpretation by the pagans. Like the scenes from the Old Testament opposite this expresses a hope of salvation.

9 (right). **The three Hebrews in the fiery furnace.** Mid-3rd century. 20 × 34½ in. (50 × 87 cm.). Painting in the Chamber of the Velatio, Catacomb of Priscilla, Rome. The story of the three young Jews cast into the flames by Nebuchadnezzar, and saved from death by the intervention of an angel illustrates another invocation for salvation.

10 (centre). **Jonah thrown to the whale.** Late 3rd century. 16 × 23 in. (*c.* 40 × 58 cm.). Vault of a crypt, Catacomb of St Peter and St Marcellinus, Rome. The story of Jonah was both an allegory of baptism and an invocation for salvation. The realistic portrayal of the bent body of Jonah and the high prow of the boat contrast with the weird conception of the whale.

11 (right). **Noah in the Ark.** 3rd century. Catacomb of St Peter and St Marcellinus, Rome. Once more this scene is symbolic of salvation with the dove bearing an olive branch in its beak. Noah is represented in the posture of an *orans*, the ark is an open coffer, *arca* in Latin.

12 (opposite). **Christ between Peter and Paul.** Late 4th century. 88 × 96 in. (213 × 243 cm.). Crypt of the Saints, Catacomb of St Peter and St Marcellinus, Rome. This later painting openly depicts a Christian subject—Christ between the two apostles above the Divine Lamb, standing on a knoll from which the four heavenly rivers flow. To the left are SS. Gorgonius and Peter, and to the right SS. Marcellus and Tiburtius. Such a decoration has monumental character.

13. **Christ Helios.** Early 4th century. Mosaic. Ceiling of a chamber from the Pre-Constantinian necropolis under the Basilica of St Peter. Here Christ appears in his glorious role—as the sun in his chariot, the Apollo of the ancients.

14 (left). **Vault mosaic.** 4th century. Sta Costanza, Rome. These are the earliest surviving vault mosaics on a large scale; they combine Christian and pagan subjects, and are enclosed in a geometric border. This detail shows a Bacchic scene, with *bacchi* gathering grapes and oxen bringing in the harvest.

15 (below). **Detail of the mosaic decoration** in the adjoining section of the ambulatory, showing the fruit and foliage and the peacock. Similar mosaics adorned contemporary pagan buildings.

16 (opposite above). **Interior of Sta Costanza, Rome.** 4th century. The magnificent mausoleum of Constantina, one of the daughters of Constantine, became a church. The vaults of the ambulatory and the apses of the beautiful circular monument are decorated with mosaics.

17 (opposite below). **The apse mosaic** in the north ambulatory shows Christ standing on a rock from which flow the four streams of Paradise. He gives the law, '*traditio legis*', to St Peter, with St Paul to his left; the sheep at his feet represent saved souls.

18 (above). **The story of Jonah.** 4th century. Detail of a floor mosaic from the basilica at Aquileia. The two scenes from the story of the prophet, his escape from the sea monster and his sleep beneath the gourd, are set against an extensive background similar to many pagan mosaics of the same time. The sea is full of realistically depicted fishes of all kinds.

19 (left). **The detail of the cupids fishing** shows how the pagan motifs were still employed side by side with Christian subjects. The octopus and swimming ducks are delightfully imaginative.

20. **Christ teaching the Apostles.** *c.* 400. Mosaic. Sta Pudenziana, Rome. This detail from the apse mosaic (see figure 22) shows the haloed Christ, 'Lord the Preserver of the church of Pudentiana', seated on his throne in full glory. Behind him is the rock of Golgotha on which is a representation of the jewelled cross which was erected there by Constantine or Theodosius.

21 (opposite). **The nave of Sta Maria Maggiore.** 432–40 (ceiling *c.* 1500). Rome. Built during the 'classical revival' under Sixtus III, the wide, majestic nave of the basilica is flanked by two aisles. The Ionic columns support a 'classical' entablature and a clerestorey and lead towards the triumphal arch which used to continue into the original apse vault. Mosaics on the arch celebrate the Virgin as the Mother of God; on the left wall of the nave are scenes from the life of Abraham and Jacob (plates 22, 23), and on the right wall, of Moses and Joshua (plates 24, 25).

22 (right). **Abraham and Lot.** Early 5th century. Mosaic. Sta Maria Maggiore, Rome. These mosaic scenes are enclosed in frames under the windows of the clerestory. This scene shows the parting of the two brothers, leading the wandering Hebrews. Abraham with his son departs to the left and Lot with his daughters to the right. Both the setting and the costumes are borrowed from classical art and there is no attempt at local colour.

23 (right). **Abraham and the angels.** Early 5th century. Mosaic. Sta Maria Maggiore, Rome. The story of Abraham with his heavenly visitors is divided into two registers: above, the patriarch greets his visitors, and below he tells his wife Sarah to make 'cakes upon the hearth', and offers them a 'calf tender and good'. It is the story of God's promise of a son to the father of his people.

24. **The passage of the Red Sea.** Early 5th century. Mosaic. Sta Maria Maggiore, Rome. This is a magnificent composition despite the limitations of the frame. To the left stand the Children of Israel led safely across the Red Sea by Moses. The Egyptian army and their chariots, leaving the citadel on the right, are engulfed in the returning waters of the sea.

25. **The capture of Jericho.** Early 5th century. Mosaic. Sta Maria Maggiore, Rome. Joshua's army march round Jericho and the walls topple; the figure within the city may be identified with the harlot Rahab who was saved because she hid the messengers who had been sent by Joshua to spy on the city. This is the upper register of a panel; below there is a procession with the trumpeters.

26. **Qalat Siman.** *c.* 470. Syria. This view shows the porch of the southern basilica of the cruciform sanctuary of St Simeon Stylites. Round the column, on the top of which the saint had spent thirty years of his life, an octagon was built, and from this radiated four basilicas each with a nave and two aisles (see figure 32). The narthex can be seen behind the arches of the porch, with typical Syrian mouldings. To the right appears the top of the central apse at the end of the eastern basilica.

27 (right). **Detail of the façade decoration** showing the fluted pilasters of the entrance porch and the magnificent capitals of spiky acanthus leaves.

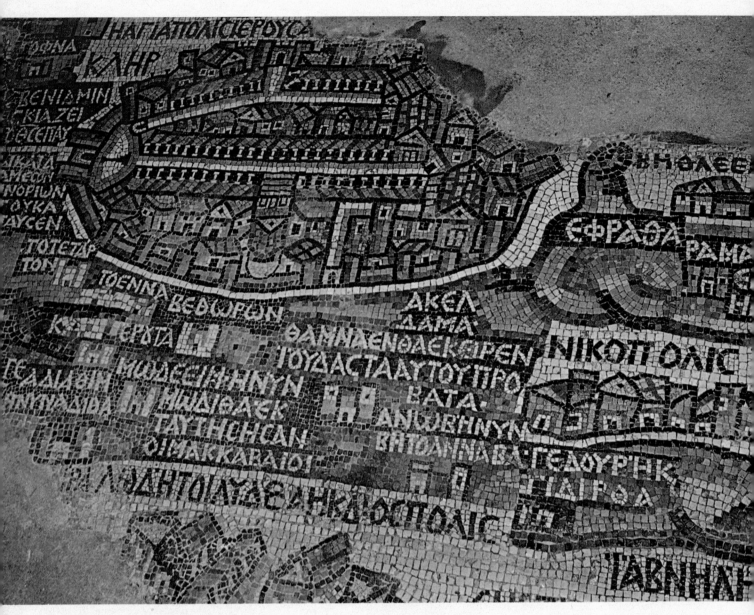

28. **Plan of Jerusalem.** *c*. 560. Mosaic.
Madaba, Jordan. The best preserved part
of the floor mosaic map of the Holy Land
is the area depicting Jerusalem, seen at the
top of this picture. Some streets and
buildings can be recognised; on the left is
the city gate, with its obelisk. From here
run two streets lined with porticoes, and
in the middle of the lower of these two can
be seen the Church of the Holy Sepulchre
(figure 15).

Constantine

THE CHURCH TRIUMPHANT

Despite the ponderous but often rhetorical account given by Eusebius of Caesarea, and despite the vengeful clamour of Lactantius, it is difficult to imagine the up-heaval that was caused in the Roman world by the triumph of Christianity. Our own time has made us familiar with revolutionaries emerging from underground, with con-demned men suddenly set free, and exiles returning home to occupy the highest posts in the State—their ideas, only a short time before subversive, suddenly becoming the law of the land. In 305, Diocletian had burned the Scrip-tures, destroyed the churches and executed the bishops in a vain attempt to preserve at all costs the unity of the empire around the emperors, who modelled themselves on Jupiter and Hercules. Suddenly full civic rights had to be granted to this community which had previously been illegal. It was even granted a kind of primacy. And to assure the unity of the empire, it was also necessary, un-fortunately, to tighten the unity of the Christians them-selves. In 325, at Nicaea, Constantine presided over the first Ecumenical Council—amidst the very bishops who had survived the repression of his predecessor. He himself, victorious through a miracle of Christ, found himself engaged for political, but perhaps also for intellectual and emotional reasons, in a theological debate. Previously, he had hesitated between paganism and Christianity; now he hesitated between the views of his advisers—orthodoxy and Arianism. Even on his death bed he was not baptised in the faith that he had proclaimed at Nicaea. The affairs of the Church had become the affairs of the State; theo-logical disputes became a question of conscience for the emperor.

At first the Christian emperors did not indulge in persecution against paganism; they attacked neither the gods they had abandoned, nor their believers. In the middle of the 4th century there was even a revival of hope on the part of the pagans when Julian, a nephew of Constantine and a Greek philosopher, became emperor. Until the end of the century there were senators in Rome, led by Sym-machus, who kept the statue of Victory in the assembly rooms—against the wishes of the Emperor Theodosius and of Ambrose, the formidable Bishop of Milan. But from the beginning the die was cast. Nothing shows this better than the building programme that is associated with Constan-tine. There were, it is true, the civil basilica of Maxentius in the Forum in Rome and Constantine's *thermae*. There was the new capital, Constantinople, built on the site of Byzantium, which was to be a new Rome—but the centre of Constantinople was the Emperor's tomb and this tomb was a church, dedicated to the twelve apostles and intended to contain their relics. Throughout the world Constantine constructed Christian sanctuaries.

Of course some of these, such as the Lateran basilica, the cathedral of the Bishop of Rome, or the octagonal church at Antioch, which was probably a Palatine chapel, do no more than represent the new alliance—the help that the empire gave the hierarchy and the help that, in turn, the empire expected from God. But a great many of these buildings take on a quite different character, expressive of Constantine's attitude to the truth of Christianity.

In Jerusalem, in answer to an appeal from Bishop Macarius and on the advice of his counsellor, Eusebius, Bishop of Caesarea of Palestine, Constantine gave permis-sion for archaeological excavations to begin. The aim was to discover the tomb of Christ—not in order to weep over the death of the Saviour, but to glorify his Resurrection. *15* The monument built on the spot would be called the *Anastasis*, the Resurrection; and the basilica adjoining it would be called the *Martyrion*, the Witness. The Church Triumphant and the Emperor both sought the historical evidence of the Resurrection—the Resurrection without which, according to St Paul, our faith would be in vain. It was during a second stage that the True Cross was dis-covered in excavations attributed to Helena, the mother of the Emperor, so Calvary was included in a secondary position in the group of buildings. The Passion found its value in the Resurrection. In Bethlehem the birthplace of Jesus was sought and found in a cave in a quarry. *17, 18*

At the summit of the Mount of Olives, a monument was built around a rock in which footprints were found that had been left by Christ before the Ascension. Other epi- *16* sodes in the earthly life of the Saviour were illustrated by the founding of sanctuaries; archaeologists have recently found, on the banks of Lake Tiberias, the sanctuary built to commemorate the miracle of the loaves and fishes. *10b*

In Rome searches were made in three places to discover traces of St Peter and St Paul. The result, *ad catacumbas*, was a basilica, now dedicated to St Sebastian, which has retained signs of a local cult of the two apostles centred around what was probably in the 3rd century a funerary

15. **The Constantinian Holy Sepulchre.** 4th century. Jerusalem. This plan of the first building of the Holy Sepulchre as reconstructed by R. P. H. Vincent is an interpretation of the description given by Eusebius, bearing in mind the few walls which have been preserved. The Holy Sepulchre was surrounded with a rotunda before the end of the century. The *propylaeum* gives access to an *atrium* before the basilica with a western apse, a nave and four aisles. A second atrium or courtyard, of which the rock of Calvary formed a corner, was in front of the vast rotunda with its internal colonnade.

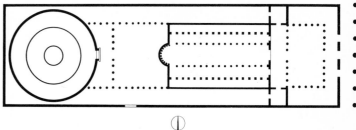

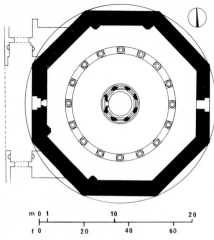

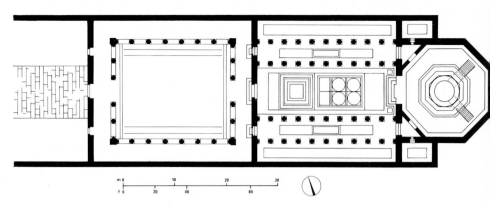

16. **Plan of the Anastasis.** 4th century. The commemorative Sanctuary of the Ascension on the Mount of Olives at Jerusalem was an octagon surrounding a rock where it was said that Christ, ascending to heaven, had left the imprint of his feet.

17. **Plan of the Sanctuary of the Nativity.** 4th century. Bethlehem. The grotto of the Nativity was covered by an octagon, and could be seen by the pilgrims through an open 'oculus' in the centre of the building. The building was completed by a large basilica which has been preserved. In the 6th century the octagon was replaced by a choir with three apses in trefoil shape.

18. **The Sanctuary of the Nativity.** 4th century. Bethlehem. Dating from the time of Constantine the colonnade of the basilica of the sanctuary is one of the earliest surviving examples of Christian architecture. Note the architraves carried by the columns.

aediculum. On the Vatican hill, after considerable levelling of the ground, a vast basilica was built around a simple monument that has just been discovered in the altar of St Peter's. S. Paolo fuori le mura is a similar case.

The authenticity of these discoveries is of little importance here. Scientific scrutiny comparable to that of our time cannot be expected of this early period and a dream held to have been inspired provided the best minds with a guarantee that may be, for us, worthless. The Holy Sepulchre, as we know from a reference made by Eusebius, owed its discovery to a dream and St Ambrose found through a dream the tomb of St Gervase and St Protase. These monuments illustrate the great work of Eusebius, the first history of the Church. What is important here is that the Christian Emperor and his advisers sought to place in time and space the earthly life of Christ and to verify and glorify the origins of Christianity.

CONSTANTINIAN CHURCH BUILDING

The help of the Emperor was indispensable to any such programme—first of all, because of the land question. In the small towns of Africa—and elsewhere—it was extremely difficult to erect a vast new basilica in the midst of a concentrated mass of urban building—the Christian community houses did not cover a large enough area of ground and were not necessarily in the town centres. The churches of the 4th century are near the outskirts of their towns. This was the price they paid for being able to develop without undue hindrance, with all the ancillary activities that the community life entailed. Similarly in Rome the monuments to the apostles—and also the martyria of other cities—were built over the cemeteries where they were buried, which were naturally outside the walls. The Lateran cathedral was built on a large estate bordered by Aurelian's wall which was given to the Bishop by Constantine, and nearby, was the church of Sta Croce in Gerusalemme. In the East the churches were more determined to give expression to their triumph. In Constantinople the church of the Holy Apostles, the church of Divine Wisdom (H. Sophia), and the church of Divine Peace, (H. Irene's) were all built within the new city; but this, of course, was an easy thing to do since they could be included in the original plans. At Antioch or Jerusalem, such a privilege involved considerable demolition. Yet a site has been discovered in the Syrian capital very near the imperial palace rebuilt by Diocletian, on the island that formed part of the monumental centre of the city. In Jerusalem, the tomb of Christ was discovered under the pagan temples in the centre of Aelia Capitolina, the city Hadrian had built on the site of Jerusalem after its destruction; it was near the tetrapyle that marked the principal crossroads.

A major difficulty was the levelling of the ground necessitated by the proposed building. The tomb of Christ was of a subterranean type well known in the East at the time and was closed by means of a heavy, circular stone (which the holy women feared they would not be

19a,b

28

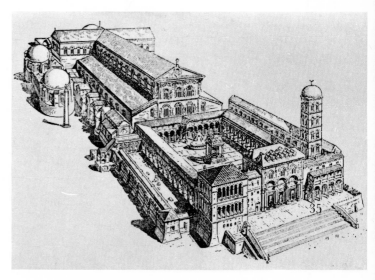

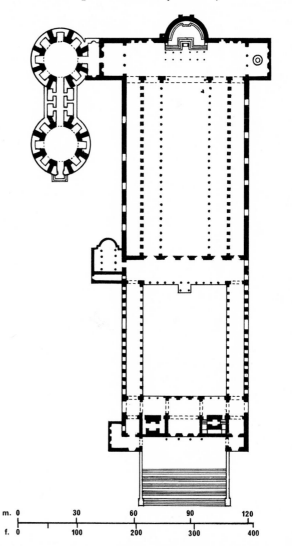

19 *a, b*. **St Peter's, Rome.** 4th century. This monument, erected by Constantine and his son, was a basilica with a nave and four aisles and a transept. The dedicatory inscription consecrates the basilica to Christ, who had allowed the Emperor to triumph over his enemies. The drawing *(a)* of the 16th century shows the basilica with all the later additions while the plan *(b)* shows the building as it was in the 4th century.

m. 0   30   60   90   120
f. 0   100   200   300   400

able to push back on the morning of the Resurrection).
It was transformed into an aediculum, around which the
sanctuary was to be built. The level of the ground was
lowered by at least twelve feet, which was a major opera-
tion involving considerable excavation. The rock of Calvary, which now looks like a cube-shaped block, was three
hundred feet south-east of the tomb and was included in
the sanctuary complex. The top of this rock, in which the
Cross had been fixed, was preserved, but the sides and surrounding area were cut straight down to the lowered level
of the ground, and a courtyard was formed with this
outcrop in the angle; even so the complex remained at a
higher level than the street. At Bethlehem, fewer altera-
17, 18 tions were needed because the Grotto of the Nativity was
kept in its natural form. A hole was made in the rock ceiling and this circular *oculus*, or small window, occupied the
centre of the commemorative octagon: the pilgrims stood
on a raised surround to look down, over a circular railing,
into the natural crypt, where the incarnation had taken
place.

19a, b   In St Peter's, Rome, excavations have shown that the
Constantinian monument had been organised around an
early, very simple, aediculum—two small columns and a
horizontal stone slab placed in front of a niche hollowed
out of the wall. This structure which was similar to certain
funerary monuments in Rome and Ostia was situated
over a rich pagan cemetery of a much later period than
the saint himself. In order to build the basilica, this cemetery had to be filled in. Moreover, the summit of the hill
(now the Vatican hill) on the slopes of which it was built,
had to be levelled off. All this involved an enormous
amount of work among the splendid mausoleums of the
necropolis, including the building of stone substructures to
support each of the columns of the sanctuary. The extent
of this work shows how the builders submitted the entire
construction of a sanctuary to the monument it commem-
orated. The results of archaeological research limited the
architect, and the glorification of the relics imposed expense on the client which could not be avoided. Whether
in Jerusalem or Rome, the holy relics were enclosed in
marble and surrounded by columns, railings and lamps.

In view of the expense involved in the preparation of
these sites, the buildings themselves might have been constructed more solidly. But it has been observed that Christian architectural forms were established at a time when
other types of buildings were constructed with elaborate
technical methods such as in the basilica of Maxentius in
the Forum. These methods were first used in the *thermae*, or
public baths—a very large hall, covered by three concrete
groined vaults, supported on both sides by lower vaults
sustaining the pillars. It was much more like a *frigidarium*
than like the pillared, wood-covered buildings that formed
the basilicas of the original Forum or even those of Trajan.
Confronted with the needs of the Christian church, the
architects were unable to exploit these innovations, so
they returned to the traditional methods, adopting styles

that were less complex, perhaps because they were cheaper.
Constantine was building a capital which was to take up
a considerable proportion of the funds available; and the
rebuilding of churches that had been destroyed in the
persecution, together with the enlargements and improve-
ments that were found necessary, required an enormous
financial programme. Even when the Emperor asked
Bishop Macarius to make plans for as magnificent a sanctuary as possible for Jerusalem, it is probable that the
money given for the work was somewhat limited. The destruction caused at Constantinople by the Nika revolt at the
beginning of the reign of Justinian does not provide an
adequate explanation for the total disappearance of Constantine's capital—perhaps it was just not built solidly
enough. In Rome St Paul's was destroyed by fire; the
ancient St Peter's had to be razed to the ground before
Michelangelo could build a new church; the Lateran
basilica was enlarged and altered several times. No trace
has been found of the octagon at Antioch; and with great
difficulty attempts are being made to find pieces of the
walls of the original Holy Sepulchre beneath the plaster-
work and rebuilding of the Crusaders. Hardly anything
remains except the fine colonnade of the sanctuary at   *18*
Bethlehem—the octagon that was constructed over the
grotto was replaced, under Justinian, by a *trefoil*, a treble
apse, and the mausoleum at Rome of one of the Emperor's
daughters, Constantina, became the church of Sta   **14, 15, 16**
Costanza. The discussion about these vanished monuments
is never-ending and controversy is increased rather than
diminished by the most methodical excavations.

André Grabar has shown that although these commemorative monuments were of very different types, the intention was the same: to serve as a shrine for some holy
place, to enable the masses to come as pilgrims and con-
template it without harming it and to assemble nearby for
communal prayer. The spectators used to arrange themselves in concentric circles around a single point. The
monuments were therefore either circular or polygonal
and resembled the imperial mausoleums, which had a
similar purpose. This was why the mausoleum of Constan-   **16**
tina, which was classified as one of the imperial tombs,
could also be classified among the Constantinian *martyria*.
It includes an internal circular portico, as later did the
sanctuary of the Ascension and the rotunda of the Holy   *15, 16*
Sepulchre. There is a development here from the round
mausoleum to the concentric sanctuary. But this type of
building could not be developed indefinitely: in fact, even
with its internal colonnade, the diameter of the rotunda   *15*
of the Holy Sepulchre is no larger than the unbroken
diameter of the dome of the Pantheon in Rome. The
architects were therefore led to combine the circular
structures with the great colonnaded rectangular halls.
The two forms could be juxtaposed, linked only by
porticos which integrated them into a single composition,
as in the churches of the Holy Sepulchre and of the Holy   *15*
Apostles at Constantinople. They could also be combined,

20. **Aquileia cathedral.** 4th century. Veneto, Italy. At the same time as vast monuments were erected with the help of the emperor to celebrate the great souvenirs of Christianity, cathedrals were being built everywhere to replace the more modest churches destroyed in the persecution of Diocletian. The earlier double church of Aquileia was replaced by a basilica with nave and two aisles with a clerestorey.

17 as was the case at Bethlehem, where the colonnades opened directly on to the octagon.

19a, b   The ecclesiastical needs that determined the design of St Peter's, Rome, were the same: a monument in which a crowd could be assembled around the tomb of the apostle and which would glorify Christ, whose first witness in Rome he had been. But the architect went further; he added to the basilica a transept, separating it from the apse, in front of which the monument of the apostle was placed at the centre of the three huge radiating areas. The basilica with transept was to have a long future, especially after the second half of the 6th century, when an altar was erected by St Gregory the Great over the tomb of St Peter —that is to say, when the difference finally disappeared between the church as community house and the commemorative monument. Several Greek basilicas and most of the churches in the West were then to become basilicas with transepts. Later the fusion of the two types of buildings chosen by the Constantinian architects, the rotunda and basilica, was to result in the basilica with dome, which became the accepted type of church in the East.

It might be said that as early as the first half of the 4th century, the first architects to deal with the requirements of the Christian church chose or created definitive solutions or prepared the elements of them, the basilica, the rotunda, and the basilica with transept. The influence of the plan of the Holy Sepulchre, or that of St Peter's was to *15, 19a, b* be perpetuated because of the fame of the sanctuaries and the artistic prestige of the architectural solutions. Throughout history, they were to serve as models. Constantine himself may not have played much part in their choice, but it was he who initiated the commissions and set the artists to work. Things really begin with him.

DECORATIVE MOTIFS

The almost total disappearance of these monuments means that there is little trace of their extremely rich decoration. Here, too, the traditions of the Roman artists were adopted without reservation and their motifs used with no concern for the symbolic interpretations that they might have had for the pagans. The decoration of the vaults of Sta Costanza is typical in this respect. They contain **14, 15** complicated geometrical patterns such as can be found in earlier or contemporary mosaic pavements. At Sousse, for example, or at Cherchel, in North Africa, there are many examples of these combinations of circles and polygons with rounded sides enclosing birds, animals, cupids or dancing-girls. Similarly, those scenes of the wine-harvest

21. **Ampulla.** 6th century. Chased silver. Cathedral treasury, Monza, Italy. Bottles such as this were brought back from Jerusalem by pilgrims, and would have contained oil of the wood of the Cross. According to tradition this one belongs to a collection offered to the Lombard queen Theodelinda in 625. It represents the scene of the Ascension of Christ, borne in a medallion by angels. Below the Virgin prays among the Apostles. The arrangement of the figures is comparable to that in the Syrian miniatures of the monk Rabula (figure 55).

that add grace and life to a large vine scroll—the loading of the ox-carts and naked peasants treading the grapes—are found throughout pagan art. The vine scrolls depict the same frolicking *putti* as before. The motif seems to have slipped without transition from its Dionysiac meaning to symbolise the Eucharist, and similar motifs can be seen in the catacombs.

Similarly, in the great mosaic of the church of Aquileia, which dates from the beginning of the 4th century, animals quite foreign to Christian symbolism are arranged in geometrical compositions. These form a framework round birds and human busts, as well as fish, the Good Shepherd and scenes that are difficult to interpret, such as the twice-repeated fight between a cock and a tortoise—the cock, we are told, symbolises Christ and the tortoise Arianism. Another section of the pavement represents a sea filled with fish, which is typical of so many Alexandrian mosaics. Here, among the traditional fishing scenes in which winged cupids hold out their lines or throw out the nets from their barges, one suddenly finds Jonah being thrown from his

ship and swallowed by a sea monster. In another corner of the pavement, one can make out the prophet asleep under the gourd. The Christian subject is here treated in the same style as in the catacombs, but is more intimately linked with the traditional decorative themes with which it is interspersed.

At the same time a truly Christian iconography seems to have developed, as can be seen at Sta Costanza, in the conches of the absidal chapel, in which Christ is seen in the sky sitting on the globe, or standing on the rock from which the four rivers of Paradise flow, giving the Law to the apostles Peter and Paul. Larger scenes of the same period are found in the catacomb paintings and on the sides of sarcophagi, depicting similar subjects, but in which the whole apostolic college participates. The monuments in Jerusalem, however, seem to have had a greater variety of themes judging by some small chased silver *ampullae*, which came from the Holy Land in the 7th century and used to contain oil sanctified by contact with the wood of the Cross, or the soil of the Holy Places. They depict a

22. **Apse mosaic, Sta Pudenziana.** End of the 4th century.
Rome. Despite a great many repairs, this mosaic is an example
of the decoration of a Roman apse of the late 4th century.
Christ (see plate 20) is enthroned among his Apostles,
accompanied by personifications of the church of the
Circumcision and the church of the Gentiles. In the background
is Golgotha, with the cross planted by Constantine or
Theodosius and the symbols of the Evangelists. The view of
Jerusalem evokes the celestial city and it has been suggested
that the rotunda to the left recalls the Sanctuary of the Holy
Sepulchre.

whole series of scenes, either singly or in groups. The iconography is sufficiently stable for one to be able to assert the
existence of well-known models, probably the paintings
and mosaics that decorated the Holy Places themselves.
These scenes include the Resurrection, with the holy women
arriving at the tomb and being met by the angel. The tomb,
as was often the case, was represented in the form of the
aediculum erected by the Constantinian architects around
the Holy Sepulchre. There is the Ascension, the Crucifixion,
the Annunciation, the Visitation, the Nativity and the Baptism of Christ. Some of these pictures were probably introduced into the monuments of the Holy Land at a later date;
but it is nonetheless possible, to recognise in some of them
at least a reflection of their original decoration.

22   The late 4th-century mosaic in the apse of Sta Pudenziana helps us to interpret the images of the *ampullae*.
20   Christ is enthroned in the centre, surrounded by the
apostles and two female figures, which are interpreted as
allegories. Behind the throne is a rock—the rock of Calvary
—surmounted by a cross, either the one planted there by

Constantine or that of Theodosius II, if the latter the
mosaic is of a slightly later date. Behind this are the monuments of Jerusalem—the sanctuaries built around the
Holy Places mentioned earlier, which here suggest the
celestial Jerusalem. In the sky appear the apocalyptic
symbols of the Evangelists.

   Such a work, which is related to the simpler works in
Sta Costanza and to the scenes depicted on the sarco- 17
phagi and in the catacombs, reveals an established iconography in which scenes from the earthly and the heavenly
lives of Christ are intermingled, as if to emphasise the two
natures he unites within his person. The second person
of the Blessed Trinity lived in Palestine under the reign of
the Emperor Tiberius. His earthly life was soon to be described, as well as the history of the patriarchs on the walls
of Sta Maria Maggiore, Rome. From now on his sovereign- 22,23,24,
ty was recognised, was shown in pictures where the Saviour 25
is enthroned in the midst of his apostles like an emperor in
his court. And the cross of suffering became, through the
emperors, the very sign of his triumph.

Basilicas and Sanctuaries

THE CHRISTIAN BASILICA

The recognition of the Christian Church by the State obviously reassured those who hesitated and the number of conversions increased. The communities already in existence expanded and new ones were rapidly created. Sooner or later all those who could afford to do so built their own churches, many of which have disappeared; but enough have survived to give an idea of their form and development. Thus in certain provinces of the Roman Empire there are are numerous well-preserved basilicas which give a better idea of the architecture of the time than the churches in the countries which remained Christian. The latter were usually enlarged and altered according to the changing demands of the liturgy or of taste, and seldom give such a complete and unadulterated picture. Places like Ravenna are important exceptions. The later Muslim invasion of Syria, for example, created a frontier over the Taurus, ruining the peasants of northern Syria, who lived solely from the cultivation of olives, by cutting them off from the buyers of their oil. They were forced to go down into the plains, abandoning their villages and churches, in order to be able to sow corn. As a result the buildings are almost the same as they were in the 7th century, apart from earthquake damage.

In examining all those buildings erected to serve the liturgical requirements of the community, one realises that during the two centuries after Constantine, throughout the whole of the Mediterranean world, they were unexpectedly similar—at least at first sight. Looking more closely at the plans of these buildings, the numerous important differences become obvious, but the resemblances dominate. All these churches are basilicas, or to be more precise, they are basilicas with three aisles, facing east, with a raised apse at the east end. The central nave is nearly always broader and higher, and is lit by a clerestory above the colonnades. In the first half of the 4th century there are a small number of basilicas in which, as in the Constantinian buildings, the columns support architraves. After some hesitation, due to reasons of economy rather than of symbolism— for the high shafts needed for architraves were very costly— arcades supported by columns were soon adopted almost everywhere.

This is a much more precise definition than that given of the Roman civil basilica, which was a rectangular pillared hall, with clerestory, often with an apse at the end of one of the smaller sides. More often, however, the building was surrounded by the colonnade on the four sides and there were many variations of it not to be found in the churches. The Christians adopted one particular type of civil basilica, perhaps influenced by the basilical halls that were to be found in the imperial palaces, or perhaps because this plan had already been thought suitable for the religious meetings of other cults, as in the famous 'Pythagorean basilica' of the Porta Maggiore, certain Mithraea, or particularly in some synagogues. It was a convenient formula and it is quite probable that it was

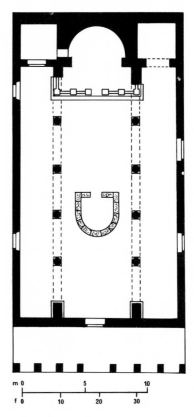

23. **Plan of the basilica at Kharab Shems.** 5th century. Northern Syria. It is in Syria that the early Christian churches have best been preserved, usually in small village parishes; they are modest but carefully built in chipped stone and timber. This church has a nave and two aisles with an eastern apse and two eastern chapels.

recommended, officially or unofficially, by imperial example—Mr Ward Perkins has shown that the cathedral at Rome, the Constantinian basilica of the Lateran, did not originally have the transept with which it was later provided in imitation of St Peter's. It could therefore have served as a prototype.

In any case, the model was adopted everywhere—often for centuries. Churches of every period, despite changes in methods of roofing, answer the same description. In the West the general appearance was to be somewhat modified by the spread of the transept, first created at St Peter's, and in the East by the introduction of the cupola and vaulting. In Syria there were façades with two towers— the ancestors of the Romanesque and Gothic façades— from the end of the 5th century.

We are not concerned here simply with architectural tradition. Once a particular type of basilica was adopted it became canonical—and was preserved even when new building techniques made some of its formulae entirely obsolete. So even in our time columns or pillars are retained in churches built of reinforced concrete which could easily be covered with a single span. It is difficult for religions and for ecclesiastical hierarchies not to regard as sacred—whether consciously or unconsciously—whatever tradition has handed down from the past.

24. The Bishop's chair in the apse.
Church of Sta Maria delle Grazie, Grado,
Italy. The apse of the 5th-century church
showing the floor mosaic which was found
almost intact under a later floor, has
preserved the circular bench *(synthronon)*
for the clergy, and the bishop's chair.
The altar used not to be in the apse.

This fidelity to tradition was all the more curious in that the basilical form was not, even from the very beginning, necessary for the performance of the liturgy. The mass was not presented as a spectacle that took place in the apse, attended by the congregregation seated in the nave and two aisles. The apse was more like a presidential tribune, with the bishop's throne placed in the centre, surrounded by a semicircular bench intended for the clergy. According to region, and sometimes in the same region, the altar occupied different places in the building. In Syria it is sometimes found against the rear wall of the apse—in which case there was obviously no *synthronon*. At other times it is placed at the front of the apse, just above the steps. In North Africa, or in Greece, it is often found in the nave immediately before the steps of the apse, or even in the middle of the central nave. The placing of the railings (chancels) which mark off the area reserved for the clergy, provides further evidence of these differences. The *ambo*, intended for readings and sermons, had various forms: sometimes it was attached to the chancel, and sometimes it was placed further into the nave. In Syria, it was replaced by a *bema*— a semicircular dais, forming a counter-apse in the middle of the nave, on which the clergy sat around a lectern for the first part of the *synaxis*. In the East, the apse, occasionally open to the nave, was usually shut off by a curtain

before being permanently cut off by the introduction of the partition known as the *iconostasis*.

In view of these variations, the congregation occupied different parts of the basilica—especially in the East where the Semitic custom of keeping the men and the women separate in the synagogue was maintained. Sometimes, as at Philippi in Macedonia, the whole nave was reserved for the movements of the clergy; they even went so far as to build galleries over the side aisles, the *matroneum*, to keep the women apart.

The apse was often isolated, projecting beyond the east end, but frequently it was completely enclosed by the eastern wall of the church. At this point two rectangular rooms were created on the right and left sides, which served as sacristies. In Syria, from the beginning of the 5th century, the one on the south side became a chapel dedicated to the relics of the martyrs. Later, in the Byzantine liturgy, they came to be called the *prothesis* and the *diaconicon* and played a necessary part in the performance of the eucharistic *synaxis*.

At a time in which the liturgy had no strict form—even within each province—the building was adapted to different needs, concurrently and successively. The basilica was not the mould which decided the form the ceremonies would take, but an adaptable hall, which the clergy

25. **The Ambo.** 5th century. Leptis Magna, Homs, Tripolitania. The ambo of the Christian basilica of Leptis Magna was constructed of capitals and marble slabs from pagan monuments. It was built on the axis of the nave of the

26. **The 'Bêma'.** 5th century. Western church at Behyo, northern Syria. Clearly seen in the centre of the nave the bêma is a semi-circular chancel which, in the Syrian liturgy, was used by the clergy during the first part of the mass for reading and preaching.

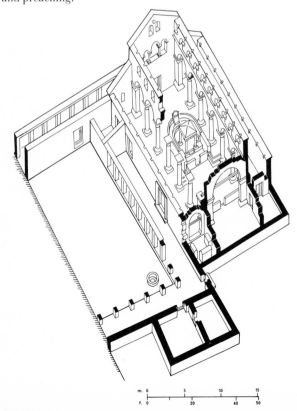

civilian basilica, which was erected by the Emperor Septimius Severus, in the town of his birthplace, and was transformed into a church under Justinian.

altered according to their own needs and tastes. This is still the case; following the recent Vatican Council for example the old basilicas are once more undergoing changes that are liturgical in origin.

It should be added that the basilica did not become the whole church all at once. For too long the Christian community had been using a house containing many different rooms. The basilica only replaced the meeting-hall and was usually surrounded by a number of other buildings, arranged around a courtyard, sometimes in front of the west façade and treated as a decorative element—the *atrium*—and sometimes on the south side, treated simply as a utilitarian addition. Among these buildings devoted to the various episcopal services were the baptistery, the catechism room (the *cathecumeneum*), chapels dedicated to the martyrs, funerary chapels and rooms which might have been used as a school, as offices and as accommodation for the bishop, the clergy and guests. Here again, there was a great deal of variation; sometimes the plans seem to have been conceived as a whole by an architect, at others one feels that the building has grown with the needs and the means of the community.

The form of the basilica was a beautiful one, on the outside and inside. It allowed interpretations such as the majestic colonnades of Sta Maria Maggiore in Rome and the church of the Nativity in Bethlehem, or the more graceful and delicate colonnades of Sta Sabina in Rome and of S. Apollinare at Ravenna. There is the complex of buil-

28

21
18

27

27. **The nave of Sta Sabina.** 422–32. Rome. The basilica is typical of the plan of the Roman basilicas of the 5th century.

The beautiful columns and capitals, perhaps from an older building, contribute to the grace and elegance of the church.

28. **Aerial view of Hippo Regius,** Algeria. The aerial view of the Christian quarter shows the basilica with its nave ending in an apse, and two aisles, surrounded by numerous dependent buildings—baptistery, chapels, courtyard, library, *triclinium* and dwellings. This was very probably where St Augustine spent his years as bishop.

dings at Jerash, in Jordan, with its *propylaea*, its two churches one after another, separated by the courtyard in which, on the feast day, the miracle of the marriage-feast at Cana was enacted and wine flowed from the fountain. The picturesque austerity of the basilicas of southern Syria was due to a special building method whereby the roofs were covered solely by lava cut into long slabs— which necessitated a series of transverse arches. Or one may prefer the charm of the small churches of northern Syria, built, like their villages, in limestone from the hills on which they stood, and in which there is a proliferation of carved decoration that covers the capitals, lintels and arcades, enriched with mouldings which run like garlands **27,** *29b* from window to window along the façades.

The Christian basilicas of the 4th and 5th centuries vary so much, both in their architectural outline and in their decoration, from Istria to Tripolitania, from Spain to *28* Macedonia, as to make the Christian art of each province worthy of separate study.

Among these provinces, there were some that followed different paths, probably because of different architectural traditions. In Asia Minor, for example, there appeared, at Binbirkilisse, the Thousand and One Churches, the first vaulted basilicas. They were of limited dimensions, with narrow aisles of almost equal size, filled with heavy pillars, which were very dark, because the builders did not dare to make a clerestory beneath the vaults. They are scarcely

29 *a, b*. **Qalb Louzeh.** *c*. 500. Syria. The exterior of the church from the north *(a)* shows the sturdy construction of the standing wall between the nave and side aisle, the regular arches of the clerestorey windows, and the rounded apse to the east. The south-west door, seen through the arch to the extreme right, is illustrated here *(b)* to show the typical elaborately carved decoration of the portal (see plate 27).

more than curiosities, but they pose the problem that was shortly to alter Christian architecture.

THE SANCTUARIES OF THE MARTYRS

It was also because of the frequent presence of vaults, and, here, of domes, that the monuments built to the glory of the martyrs have a particular architectural importance. Before the *Pax Ecclesiae*, the rites with which they had been honoured in the cemeteries had been of a discreet kind; the community honoured their martyrs in the same way as the families honoured their dead. But with the triumph of the Church, things became quite different. Each church was proud of its martyrs, and believing with some justification that the list was now complete, a liturgical calendar was drawn up, and each saint was celebrated on the anniversary of his death. The Church also began to honour them with sanctuaries which grew in size and wealth in order to receive the crowds who came on pilgrimage.

At Salona particularly, but also at Trier in Gaul, or Tipasa in Mauretania, the development of the monuments may be traced from the simple tomb, more or less decorated and enlarged, to the mausoleum and sanctuary. Even in Rome, on the spot said to be '*ad catacumbas*', there existed in the 3rd century only a very simple monument surrounded by a courtyard onto which opened a hall intended for funeral feasts. We know from graffiti that this group of buildings was connected with the cult of St Peter and St Paul. After the *Pax Ecclesiae*, these buildings were filled up and over them was built a vast basilica, in the form of a Roman circus, with a nave that was possibly not covered. In Rome, basilicas were built over the catacombs to allow the crowds to honour the martyr buried in the gallery beneath. At Salona one can see the development of basilicas, either covered or not, from an *exedra*-shaped mausoleum. Other vaulted, two-storeyed tombs provide a hall for devotion over the funerary hall. But also at Salona a cruciform church soon developed, built according to the usual methods used in basilicas.

Here and there other forms appeared, sometimes linked, as in the time of Constantine, with basilicas: the same

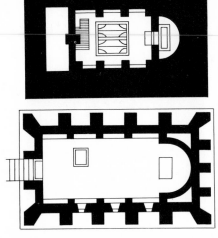

30. **Plan of martyria, cemetery of Marusinac.** 5th century. Salona, Dalmatia. The tombs of the martyrs were covered with a large mausoleum or even a basilica, sometimes preceded by porticos. Several sanctuaries were grouped together in a cemetery with a courtyard and a few tombs of devout christians.

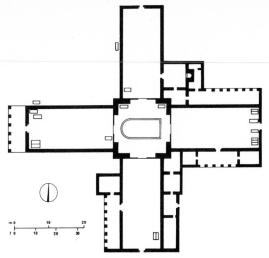

31. **Martyrion of St Babylas.** 381. Antioch-Kaoussié, southern Turkey. The cruciform monument was erected round the tomb of the martyr-bishop Babylas. It has no apse; the focal point of worship was in the central square, where a platform for the clergy was placed next to the sarcophagus of the saint. Bishop Meletios, who built the church, also wished to be buried there.

lateral treble apse is to be found at Corinth and Tebessa; isolated, in Jerusalem, it forms the *martyrion* of St John the Baptist. At Mount Nebo we find it over the 'Tomb of Moses'; in the White Monastery at Sohag, in Egypt, it replaces the apse. In Armenia, the *quatrefoil* (with four apses) is found in several places, at Bagaran and Vagarshapat, modern Echmiadzin, but there is also one at Tsaritchingrad, in Serbia.

The quatrefoil can also become an open baldachin, or canopy, with pillars and columns surrounding the apses. On the outside the monument containing it might reproduce its shape, or keep to a more simple outline, a rotunda, for example. Trefoil monuments are to be found in Syria, at Seleucia Pieria, Apamea, Bosra and later at St Sergius' at R'safah. But there was also one in Athens, in Hadrian's *stoa* and another at Perustica, in Bulgaria. Perhaps the oldest example of the series is to be found in

49 Milan, at S. Lorenzo. It is also the most monumental, the most faithful to Roman building methods—the one in which the derivation from the mausoleums of imperial Rome is most apparent, despite the new developments of the plans. But all these buildings had to face the very delicate problems of the joining of the vaults—though in different terms according to the form of the exterior shell. Even more than the balance of the cupola, which was sometimes quite light, or was even replaced by a pyramidal or circular wooden roof, it was the work of these complex collaterals, often repeated on a higher storey, that forced the architects to innovate.

The development of more simple forms is also apparent. In 381, at Kaoussié, on the outskirts of Antioch, Bishop

31 Meletios had a great cruciform *martyrion* built in honour of his predecessor, St Babylas, martyred under the Emperor Decius. It was a square with sides fifty feet long formed by four arches, a *tetrapyle*, similar to those that were built at crossroads. Backing on to these arches were four halls each eighty feet long, forming a free cross, the branches orientated to north, south, east and west. This monument was not vaulted—unlike the mausoleum of Galla Placidia at Ravenna, which has an analogous scheme

in miniature. This plan was to be developed elsewhere, first at Ephesus, where, over the tomb of St John, around a square monument with four arches similar to the one at Antioch-Kaoussié, four basilicas were built to form a cross. The monument, orientated, looked somewhat like a basilica with projecting transept. On the other hand, at Qalat Siman, in northern Syria, around the column at the **26,27** top of which St Simeon Stylites had lived for thirty years, an eight-arched octagon was erected and, on this octagon, four radiating basilicas each with a nave and two aisles *32a,b* were built. It is not known whether the octagon was covered or not: it has even been suggested that there was a quatrefoil. Around this vast, complex and cleverly constructed monument some fine monastic buildings were erected, a baptistery and adjoining churches. At the foot of a triumphal way, leading from the valley and punctuated at intervals by arches, was an entire pilgrimage town with monasteries and hostelries. This magnificent group of buildings, still remarkably well preserved, was the most ambitious and the most successful example of Christian architecture before H. Sophia, Constantinople. St Simeon Stylites had died in 459 and the construction of the sanctuary was started soon afterwards. Such a building is indicative of the honour which was paid to the ascetics, who were now accorded in part the veneration formerly given to the martyrs by the masses. The body of St Simeon had been brought back to Antioch to protect the city, whose walls had been destroyed by an earthquake in 458. It is possible that the Emperor Zeno encouraged the building of a sanctuary around the column in an attempt to re-establish union between the Christians which he sought at the same time through his *Henotikon*, or Edict of Peace.

BAPTISTERIES

Apart from the *martyria*, a study of those buildings with a centralised plan should include the baptisteries, which were never developed in so monumental a way. The baptistery remained the centre of one of the fundamental ceremonies of an expanding and converting Church. On Easter night the adult catachumens gave proof of their

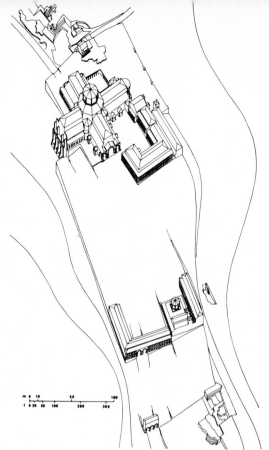

32. *a, b.* **Qalat-Siman.** 459–480. Syria. The sanctuary and the convent of St Simeon Stylites. *(a)* The reconstructed view of the complex in about 500 is after a drawing by Georges Tchalenko. Above are the stone quarries, then the great cruciform monument radiating from the octagon *(b)* erected round the column where the saint lived for thirty years. To the

right the porticoed buildings of the monastery. Below the dome of the baptistery is flanked by a side basilica, and other guest buildings. The monumental gates mark the beginning of the sacred way which descends to the valley, where a pilgrimage town developed with convents and hostelries (plates 26, 27).

religious preparation, recited the symbol of the faith and were brought before the bishop for the initiation ceremony. They were plunged naked into the bath three times, were then anointed and, dressed in white, admitted to the eucharistic office. Around the bath used for the immersion, which was often covered by a stone canopy, the baptisteries were square or circular, with a trefoil or cruciform plan. Like the *martyria*, they introduced the use of domes, which, as can be seen at Djemila in Algeria or at Salona in Dalmatia, break the linear uniformity of the roofs of the basilicas, porticos and outbuildings. Within a definite programme and with traditional forms that were to be found everywhere, the early Christian architects were still able to express their own personalities.

It should be noted that in all these monuments, the dome and a centralised plan on the one hand, or basilica, on the other, are juxtaposed, or combined, but never mixed. Each element retains its own system of construction. Even in the basilicas with transept, the existence of perpendicular aisles does not present the problem of covering a central square: the rectilinear roof of the transept is perpendicular to that of the nave which rests against it.

Two non-architectural factors were to compel the architects of the end of the 5th century to face the problem of the dome.

The first of these was the introduction of the cult of the martyrs into the parish church, and even into the cathedral. For a long time, mass had been said in the *martyria* of the cemeteries. The merging of the two cults resulted in the

disappearance of the differences between the two types of building, which, in any case, had never been completely divorced. The church became a *martyrion* and the *martyrion* became a church and the two tended to become similar. At Antioch-Kaoussié there is no east apse, whereas both *31* Ephesus and Qalat Siman have one. **26,** *32a, b*

The second factor was the discovery of the cruciform plan. Sanctuaries had always been built in the form of a cross, whether the branches appeared outside or merely inside the building, The branches naturally resulted from the buttresses which were necessary to pillars supporting a dome. Similarly, the transept of St Peter's formed a cross. *19a, b* But one cannot be at all sure that this fact was conscious. In pagan architecture there had been many buildings, *thermae* or mausoleums, based on a cruciform plan, to which no one had dreamed of giving a symbolic value. It was at the end of the 4th century that the bishops—St Ambrose was perhaps the first—thought of the symbol: **50** *Forma Crucis templum est.* The temple is in the form of a cross; the temple is the Sign of the Cross.

Thus the expansion of the transept, and the introduction of the dome at the centre of the basilica were given a religious reason and value. The basilica was retained, but it now ended not in the apse, but in a square, preceding the apse, with projecting perpendicular arms to the north and south and that square was ready to receive the Byzantine dome. And it was the Byzantine dome, with its weight and thrust, that was to alter entirely the methods and forms of Christian architecture in the East.

Ravenna and Mosaics

In order to get a first-hand understanding of the Christian art of the 5th and 6th centuries, one can do no better than go to Ravenna. This refuge city in the marshes bordering the Adriatic, owed its fortune to Augustus, who made its port Classis the base of the Adriatic fleet. At the beginning of the 5th century, the Emperor Honorius settled there and it was his sister, Galla Placidia, who, governing the state for her son, Valentinian III, from 425 to 450, gave the city the appearance of a capital. Theodoric, the Gothic chieftain, who, with the agreement of Constantinople, became king of Italy, also took up residence there and continued to embellish it. At the time of the Justinian conquest, Belisarius made Ravenna the capital of the exarchate that represented the Byzantine State in the West. The local development of architecture and of the art of mosaic shows the mixture of Italian traditions and eastern influences. The relative importance of one or the other in a particular work, or in Ravenna as a whole, will always be open to discussion. It is at all events one of the most successful and easily studied examples of Christian art.

For ten centuries mosaic was to be the decoration of the eastern churches. At Ravenna, the mosaicists had to solve all their problems—technical, decorative, figurative and iconographical. Little is known of the extent to which mural mosaics were used before the 4th century, though extraordinarily rich and magnificent collections of pavement mosaics have survived. The development of this art can be traced from its origins in Greece, whence it became so extraordinarily popular throughout the Roman empire. Recent discoveries have enabled the study of the pavement *33* mosaics of the 4th century—in Syria, in Africa and, above all, at Piazza Armerina, the great Sicilian villa, where the Emperor Maximian, the partner of Diocletian, is said by some to have retired after the voluntary dissolution of the tetrarchy in 305. We know nothing of the walls of this building, nor of many African villas of the same period, yet it seems that the fresco was still the normal method of mural decoration. However, surprises are always possible —at Pompeii, for example, mosaic was used only in the decoration of fountains. In the 4th century it is sometimes used in funerary monuments, as in the Christ-Helios or *13* Sun Christ, in one of the mausoleums discovered beneath St Peter's in Rome and, also, this time in a really monumen- *14,15* tal way, in the mosaics of the vaults of Sta Costanza.

There does not appear to have been any break: the decorative motifs of Sta Costanza as we have seen are directly related to the composition of the floor mosaics of the time. Later the first difference was in the increased use of glass cubes. The mosaicists obviously limited the use of these for floors for reasons of permanence—golden cubes for jewels, red or blue cubes for the plumage of certain birds, and sometimes blue and green cubes for the sea. As might be expected, these cubes proved too fragile and have generally disappeared.

This limitation was no longer necessary in mural mosaic.

33. **Floor mosaic of the seasons.** 4th century. Antioch, Turkey. This typical composition of scenes radiating round a central portion was later adopted in mosaic decoration of vaults. This shows the tradition of floor mosaics which, used in the time of Constantine was influenced by classical models and in turn influenced later Christian mosaicists.

34. **Decoration of the vault of the Pantheon.** *c.* 120. Rome. The panelled relief decoration is typical of the Roman solution to the problem of decorating the vault.

35. **Exterior of S. Vitale.** 546–548. Ravenna. The outer octagon is clearly distinguished in this view, and rising above it the central octagon which surrounds the dome. On the right the aisle is broken by the perpendicular roof of the presbyterium. The triple-arched window rises above the apse surrounded by its complex symmetrical dependent chapels. There is no external embellishment, the brick walls being divided only by light buttresses (see plates 40, 41).

White backgrounds made of limestone or marble were replaced first by blue then by gold, giving a splendid brilliance, the quality of light found in the interiors of Byzantine churches, and first found at Ravenna. The blue effect of the mausoleum of Galla Placidia, enriched by the golden glow from the alabaster plaques of the windows, reveals a new sensitivity and feeling for colour. Surely the Roman monuments, with their plastic panelled decoration, enclosing painted motifs in deep mouldings, could not have produced anything like these mosaics. We are now in an architecture of bricks and plaster and it is almost always strips of mosaic and not mouldings that are used to accentuate the structure of the buildings.

The mosaicists were now confronted with surfaces to decorate—or rather with all the solid areas of the interior, in the midst of which the spectator stands. Already in Ravenna they seemed to delight in varying these surfaces and masses. There were Christian basilicas of the normal type, with columns, clerestory, beamed roofs and vaulted apse in the form of a half-dome, and monuments with a centralised plan—the domed polygonal baptisteries and the cruciform mausoleum of Galla Placidia, with groined and barrel vaults. The culmination of this, the fully Byzantine monument, is the octagon of S. Vitale, which is incomparably light and still has intact, in its *presbyterium*, all its mosaic decoration. So there were not only expanses of wall to decorate but also walls broken up by windows and blind arcades, semicircular tympana and hemispherical apses, vaults and domes all posing complicated, but exciting problems for the imagination of the decorators.

Of course, the basic solutions to the different problems were not necessarily discovered in the workshops at Ravenna. Many of them had already been found and the corresponding motifs chosen—in the Christian catacomb paintings or sarcophagi, in monumental Roman art and even in earlier times. Ever since the Assyrians, if not before, the motif of the procession had been adapted by artists into a rectangular composition where figures of equal height followed each other in a direction determined by the axis of the monument. The motif of the military procession was followed by that of a triumphal procession

(Continued on page 65)

29 (opposite). **The Empress Theodora.** 6th century. Mosaic. S. Vitale, Ravenna. The pale gazing face of Theodora, with her enormous staring eyes, appears surrounded with the precious stones of her diadem, earrings and necklaces worked in mother-of-pearl. The whole representation is imbued with imperial hierarchism. The glory of Ravenna and the spirit of the Byzantine era are captured in this majestic portrait of the Empress.

37,38,39

34

30,31,42

37

35

39

40,41

30 (above). **St Apollinare in Classe.**
Classis, near Ravenna. The church was
consecrated in 549 by Maximian, the first
Archbishop of Ravenna following the
Byzantine reconquest. This view shows the
square projection at the end of the
narthex, the simple exterior of the
northern aisle with its clerestorey and the
later campanile.

31 (below). **Interior of St Apollinare
Nuovo.** *c.* 490. Ravenna. The basilica of
St Apollinare Nuovo was built by
Theodoric. It has the normal interior
with a nave, two side aisles and an apse.
The columns carry arches, above which is
the clerestorey. The panelled ceiling
hides the beams of the roof.

32 (above). **The Procession of Martyrs.**
5th–6th centuries. Mosaic. St Apollinare
Nuovo, Ravenna. This view shows the
decoration of the south wall. Over the
arches is a mosaic frieze of the procession
of the martyrs, leading to the enthroned
Christ at the east end. Above, between the
windows of the clerestorey, are figures of
saints represented like statues in niches;
over each window is a mosaic from the
narrative cycle of Passion scenes.

33 (below left). **The healing of the
paralytic.** Early 6th century. Mosaic.
St Apollinare Nuovo, Ravenna. The
narrative scenes above the north
clerestorey windows depict Christ's early
miracles. The healing of the paralytic
follows the scheme of the original
iconography of the sarcophagi, with
Christ and an apostle to the right and to
the left the miraculously healed man,
carrying his bed on his back.

34 (below right). **The Last Supper.** This
iconography was to be of long duration.
Christ, with Peter beside him, Judas
opposite and the other apostles recline
round a semicircular table, of the sort that
used to seat thirteen Romans.

35 (above). **The separation of the goats from the sheep.** Early 6th century. Mosaic. St Apollinare Nuovo, Ravenna. Another scene from the north wall, a monumental composition with a beardless Christ, enthroned between two angels. This is a prefiguration of the Last Judgment.

36 (below). **The Pharisee and the publican.** Early 6th century. Mosaic. St Apollinare Nuovo, Ravenna. As in the parable the two men pray in the temple, the Pharisee on the right and the humble publican asking forgiveness on the left. The simple presentation in no way detracts from the powerful expression.

37 (opposite). **The Mausoleum of Galla Placidia.** Mid 5th century. Ravenna. In contrast with the narrative scenes opposite, the mosaic decoration of the cross-shaped mausoleum continues uninterrupted over the whole of the upper surface. The architectural divisions are indicated by borders of mosaic garlands and geometric patterns. Dedicated to St Lawrence it contained the sarcophagi of Honorius, Galla Placidia and her husband Constantius III. Grey marble revets the lower part of the walls.

38 (above). **The Good Shepherd.** Mid-5th century. Mosaic. Mausoleum of Galla Placidia, Ravenna. Over the door is the familiar pastoral scene of the Good Shepherd with his flock. Close to classical art and the catacomb paintings, this representation differs only in the strong, graceful, if rather cold execution. The colours blend with the ensemble and the magnificent decoration of the vault above · (figure 36).

39 (below). **St Lawrence.** Mid-5th century. Mosaic. Mausoleum of Galla Placidia, Ravenna. On entering the mausoleum this lunette is seen directly opposite the door. The scene has given rise to discussion, but it is without doubt St Lawrence carrying the Bible and the Cross, and the cupboard for the Gospel books to the left. Beneath the alabaster window the rack of his torture is depicted.

40 (above). **The vault of the presbyterium of S. Vitale.** 546–548. Ravenna. Four arches, one decorated with medallions of Christ and the apostles, support a groined vault; the angels standing amidst the foliated decoration bear in triumph the central wreath of the Blessed Lamb.

41 (following pages). **Interior view of S. Vitale.** 546–548. Ravenna. The magnificent great arches of the church enclose the lighter arcatures of the ambulatory, and the presbyterium (foreground), giving the monument an effect of space and lightness. The column shafts and capitals were imported from the workshops of the Marmara islands and also, probably, the plan of the building and the methods of construction from Constantinople.

42 (opposite). **Detail of the robes of Theodora's attendant.** 546–548. Mosaic. South-west wall of the presbyterium of S. Vitale, Ravenna. The mantle is woven with a geometric pattern, and the plain dress beneath has borders embroidered with flowers. The colours and the skilful placing of the *tesserae* can here be seen to full effect.

43. **The Empress Theodora and her suite.** 546–548. Mosaic. South-west wall of the presbyterium of S. Vitale, Ravenna. Theodora and her attendants advance in stately procession towards the Christ represented in the apse. She carries a jewelled chalice and is surrounded by stately regalia. Two dignitaries precede her into the church in front of which stands an elaborate fountain. The noble, huge-eyed faces and magnificent colours are the essence of the glorious art of Byzantium.

44 (above). **The Emperor Justinian and his suite.** 546–548. Mosaic. Northeast wall of the presbyterium of S. Vitale. Ravenna. Facing the group of Theodora and her suite is this procession of Justinian accompanied by ecclesiastical dignitaries, high officials and guards. The Archbishop Maximian holds a jewelled cross, and the head behind him has been said to be that of a wealthy banker Julianus, who was in charge of the building of the church. The regality of the scene is strikingly typical of court art compared to the mosaics in the other parts of the building. Note the accuracy of the ceremony, the life-like portraits and the decorative effect of the whole.

45 (opposite). **Part of the vault mosaic of the Baptistery of the Orthodox.** 5th century. Mosaic. Ravenna. This central portion of the vault mosaic shows the *Baptism of Christ* in the central medallion, with the surrounding procession of the apostles. The frontal faces belie the movement of the robes and the placing of the apostles' feet.

46. **The Transfiguration.** *c.* 540.
Mosaic. The apse of the Church of the
Virgin in the Monastery of St Catherine,
Mount Sinai. The superb mosaic remains
untouched since Justinian's day, as are
the original carved beams of the roof,
which carry dedicatory inscriptions.
The iconography of the Transfiguration
recurs for many centuries: the apostles in
medallions under the arch are like those
at Ravenna (plate 40); here and there the
presence of Byzantine artists seems
certain.

47. **View of the golden dome of Hagia Sophia.** *c.* 563. Mosaic. Constantinople. The magnificent mosaic dome of the basilica was first constructed in 537. It collapsed in 558, and was replaced by the present dome, which suffered damage in 939 and 1346. Despite these misfortunes the glorious vault which soars above the majestic spaces of the nave remains superbly impressive.

moving towards a god or a king seated on his throne, surrounded perhaps by dignitaries. The frieze of the Parthenon was a free variation of this theme—the gods, on the west side, received the procession of the Panathenaeas, the two columns of worshippers who, after regrouping in the east, had advanced towards them through the north and south. This traditional theme was used to magnificent effect at St Apollinare Nuovo where, setting out from the two towns of Ravenna and Classis, the martyrs and saints move from the porch to the apse to offer their crowns to Christ and to the Virgin. It is curious that the Byzantine artist in the 6th century should have rediscovered the taste for strict repetition and colour that is so apparent in the procession of archers at Persepolis. His technique is certainly his own and the effect he produces, but the basic theme is inherited. The circular processions of the Egyptian zodiacs seem to be the forerunners of the procession of apostles arranged round the central medallion of the baptistery dome.

Again at St Apollinare Nuovo historical pictures were placed in panels above the clerestory. Similarly at Sta Maria Maggiore half a century earlier; perhaps the Christians may have been reviving the tradition of basilical decoration where the architectural form determined the decorative scheme. The apostles and prophets between the windows, with magnificent red and gold conches over their heads are reminiscent of the classical arrangement of statues in niches. The whole of this arrangement seems to be an attempt to reproduce a relief decoration in two dimensions. The decoration of the apses, too, was already outlined as can be seen at Sta Pudenziana, and for which there may be evidence in Palestine. At S. Vitale and at St Apollinare in Classe it consists of a triumphal scene taking place in the sky—the triumph of Christ or of a saint in a symbolic or figurative scene of Paradise. This type of representation, involving a frontal view of the principal figure, and the symmetry of the supporting figures and of the decoration, has the advantage, at the end of the church, of presenting a devotional image with remarkable dramatic effect. It is found throughout Byzantine art and even when the painting depicts a definite scene, the Transfiguration in the apse of the church of the monastery on Mount Sinai for example, the frontality and symmetry are retained.

THE DECORATION OF THE VAULT

The composition of the basilica with the distribution of

48. **Capital from Hagia Sophia.** 6th century. Marble. Constantinople. This beautiful example of a Byzantine capital, with the monogram of Justinian, the lacy, openwork design of acanthus leaves, the scrolls, and the floral motif of the abacus, is an exquisite detail typical of the magnificence of the whole basilica. The marble probably came from the quarries of the Marmara islands, as did that for the capitals and columns of S. Vitale, Ravenna (plates 40, 41, figure 97).

spaces and masses and the existence of a roof independent of the decorative scheme means that the decoration is usually rather fragmentary. But with the rise of the vault, mosaic takes over and the building gains a new unity. Whether at Galla Placidia, in the archiepiscopal chapel, in the baptisteries or in the presbyterium of S. Vitale, we are now confronted with an overall decoration which seems to have a greater unity as all the demarcations are integrated into the whole, the bands round the arches and the windows with their columns and mouldings. Individually treated figures now tend to disappear. Certain figures, integrated into gilt foliage, as at Galla Placidia, have lost any identity they ever had. Others, whose visual traits were fixed by tradition are only noticed and recognised at second glance; they look at first sight like patches of colour, whose value is dependent on the overall scheme. The side walls of the presbyterium of S. Vitale are decorated almost entirely with a background of stylised rocks, foliage, flowers and animals, all exquisitely drawn. Into this are set the figures of prophets, which are so well integrated into the lavish decoration that they are hardly noticeable despite their representing specific episodes, such as Moses tying his sandals. In the same way on the vault the angels, bearing the wreath which encircles the triumphant Lamb of Christ, become focal elements of the decorative foliage around them. The architecture itself is not merely accentuated by the colours covering it, but seems to have been interpreted anew.

FACES AND FORMS IN MOSAICS

Yet as soon as one pauses to look at them, the figures assume their real importance once again. The period covered by the Ravenna monuments is particularly instructive in the development of the representation of the human figure. Comparing the two groups of apostles or the two medallions representing the baptism of Christ in the baptisteries of the Orthodox and of the Arians, and comparing the prophets between the windows and the procession of martyrs in St Apollinare Nuovo, one is confronted with the same profound change. Ever since the 5th century, the stylisation of draperies had been very accentuated, but the faces were still treated as if they were painted portraits, with extreme subtlety in the shape and arrangement of the *tesserae*, in the tones, the shading and the placing of highlights.

Far from there being a tendency to simplification or decadent clumsiness in the 6th century, there was a new style, better adapted to monumental decoration, and which proceeded from a new spirit. In the drapery, for example, there is practically no attempt at modelling or colour shading; they are purely indicated by a play of lines that is intended to suggest both the movement of the material and the muscles it covers. In fact, this use of the contrast of black motifs against a light background is a colour effect. This is seen even more clearly when the toga is replaced by the *chlamys* and plain white material by

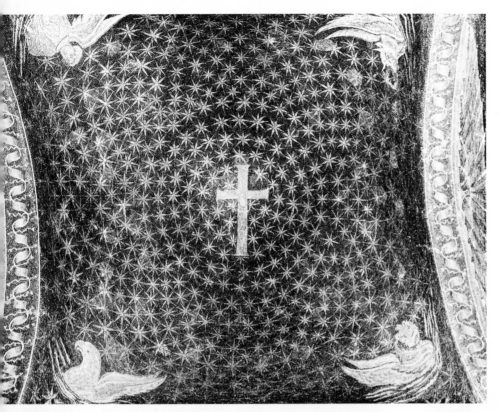

36. **Central vault of Galla Placidia.**
5th century. Mosaic. Ravenna. The cross
in a starry sky, with the symbols of the
Evangelists on the pendentives is a simple
evocation of the apocalypse. Below the
Apostles raise their heads in acclaim
(see plate 37).

37. **The Baptism of Christ.** 6th century.
Mosaic. The vault of the baptistery of the
Arians, Ravenna. The processional
composition of the Apostles giving homage
to the symbolic throne of Christ around
the baptismal scene sets theological and
liturgical themes in an architectural
setting. The rhythm of the composition,
and robust character of the monumental
decoration are noticeable.

38. **The vault mosaic.** *c.* 500. Chapel of
the Archbishop's palace, Ravenna. The
setting of the subject in the architecture
is characteristic. The angels carrying the
medallion with the cross are descended
from Roman triumphal art. The symbols
of the Evangelists occupy the spaces.

39. **Presbyterium of S. Vitale.** 546–548. Ravenna. The interior of the octagon shows how the graceful cupola is carried by the apsidal chapels with their two storeys of columns. The mosaic decoration covers the whole surface of the presbyterium, see plate 41.

40. *a, b.* **St Peter.** Ravenna. The two figures of St Peter, *(a)* from the Baptistery of the Orthodox (5th century) and *(b)* from the Baptistery of the Arians (6th century), stand in a classical setting. The supple draping of the robes, the traditional beard and the modelling of the face are almost identical in both representations.

brightly coloured trimmings and brocades. The indication of folds becomes increasingly sketchy; otherwise they would detract from the harmony and continuity of the splendid, faithfully reproduced motifs of Byzantine fabrics. It is this, at Ravenna, that makes the astonishing contrast

31 between the two processions of St Apollinare Nuovo in which the magnificent robes of the saints' court dress are presented as red surfaces, whereas the martyrs retain a certain relief, despite the simplicity with which the folds in their white togas are drawn. It is to this that the two

43,44 famous pictures in S. Vitale depicting Justinian and Theodora bringing their gifts to the church owe their strangeness and magnificence. However characteristic the

29 faces of the Emperor, the Empress, the bishop and their followers may be, what strikes one first is the incomparable brilliance of the coloured surface in which the splendour of the ecclesiastical vestments and the richness of the court costumes blend in a kind of marvellous tapestry.

But this is not all. Contrary to appearances, the subjects of these two pictures are not static. They are not groups of motionless figures who have posed for the artist, but here again processions, groups of walking figures, who, in different settings, move towards the triumphant Christ at the end of the apse, although this movement almost disappears in the stiffness of the costumes and the frontality of the figures. This is an artistic tradition which is quite foreign to the Roman West and which originated in the Hellenised East where the traditions Alexander took with him as far as the frontiers of India had developed according to their own rules and resulted in artistic forms that are quite different from their European sources. These forms —which are more familiar to us since the excavations at Dura in Mesopotamia—have since been recognised and analysed. They form what Michael Rostovtzeff called Parthian art and they had a decisive influence on Byzantine painting.

Of course, the faces are transformed—and it is this that makes the strongest impression. The frontality often creates a total symmetry in the figures: the head, seen completely in full face, is divided into two by a nose that is still sometimes given side shadow but is more often shaded equally on either side. The nose tends to disappear altogether and the face is no longer seen in relief which is no more important. The eyes now play the essential role; enlarged, sym-

29 metrical, gazing fixedly and accentuated by the thick arch of the dark shaded eyebrows, they stare pitilessly at the spectator, creating the impression of a living, supernatural presence. It is easy to understand how such figures became objects of devotion and icons. Perhaps at first this was simply the result of a technique of representation, as in the funeral portraits of the Faiyum which in the second century AD replaced the relief masks on mummies. But the effect produced is one that was later to be much sought after—and of which Byzantine spirituality was to make full use.

However, these staring faces, with their enlarged eyes, have lost nothing of their character. The eastern mode of representation certainly captures their personality in a different way and to some extent idealises them. The round, ruddy, unhandsome face of Justinian takes on a **44** certain majesty, but nonetheless remains of this world. And the difference between the portraits of Bishop Maximianus and of the figure whom some scholars have tried to recognise as Julius Argentarius, who had been in charge of the building of the church, and the more anonymous faces of the women and guards is a good indication of the degrees of stylisation that were still possible. It is not only in the cut and colour of their beards that St Peter and St Paul **40a,b** stand out from among the other apostles and from each **41a,b,c** other. The Byzantine mosaicist can still portray indivi- **41d,e** duals within the limitations of the stylised type.

There are also many occasions when the figures are not fixed in a frontal position for the sake of symmetry, whether in the processions or in one of the more active scenes. Some of the faces are, of course, entirely in profile, but even before the 6th century there was a tendency towards a frontal attitude in many of the faces. The martyrs of St Apollinare Nuovo, for example, whose **32** walking movement is subtly indicated by the slant in the hems of their cloaks or by the dissymmetry of their veils, are shown almost full face with their haloes giving the effect of so many medallions, so that the inflection of the eyes is what gives the movement to the head and even to the body.

Nevertheless, with the triumph of these tendencies we enter a new aesthetic, in which realism and respect for volumes and forms gives place to colour and vision. It is a two-dimensional world, suitable for expression and symbolism. These hieratic figures surround the worshippers, whose eyes are caught by theirs, with supernatural presences.

At Ravenna the eastern contribution did not arrive on virgin soil, but was superimposed on and modified by western traditions to which Christian art had already adapted. This is what gave the art of Ravenna its particular flavour—under the auspices of the Imperial State and of the needs of the Church.

CHRISTIAN NARRATIVE SCENES

It was inside these monumental buildings and according to this new aesthetic that the artists of Ravenna were to treat the Christian subjects of their commissions.

It is curious that at Ravenna religious history—the Old and New Testaments—seems to have been relegated to second place. It finds its essential expression in the two series of small scenes placed high up between the windows of St Apollinare Nuovo. This part of the decoration dates **32,34** from Theodoric's time and it is not surprising to find in a number of scenes the direct influence of primitive Christian art as we know it to have existed in Rome in the catacomb paintings and sarcophagi. In the representations of Christ's miracles, the man sick of the palsy, the woman **33**

41 *a, b, c, d, e.* **Mosaic portraits of St Paul in Ravenna.** 5th and 6th centuries *(a)* The Mausoleum of Galla Placidia, *(b)* the Archiepiscopal chapel, Baptisteries, *(c)* of the Orthodox, and *(d)* of the Arians, *(e)* S. Vitale, the similarity of these pictures shows that the physical appearance of the Apostle had been firmly established not only by a sufficiently precise description but by the model which was thus reproduced.

with the issue of blood, and the raising of Lazarus, the composition is the same as on the sarcophagi. Here too the Saviour, beardless, stands apart, in semi profile, followed by only one disciple, with, in front of him, the group surrounding the subject of the miracle, identifying it by their attitudes. Here and there, the composition varies: for the miracle of the loaves and fishes, the prefiguration of the Eucharist, and for the separation of the goats from the sheep, a sign of the Last Judgement, it suddenly takes on a symmetrical form and an entirely new grandeur.

On the other wall, among the scenes of the Passion, one passes directly from the betrayal of Judas to the Resurrection: as in the older art, there was no question of representing Christ as humiliated, buffeted, crucified and taken down from the cross. The holy women arrive at once at the tomb and Thomas seeks in Christ's side the tangible proof of the Resurrection, and in so doing hands it on to us. Two scenes in this series have a particular charm the parable of the Pharisee and the publican, and the denial of St Peter, in which the artist suddenly found a quite personal vitality, a taste for life, which is only found in the other scenes among the secondary figures, overshadowed as they are by the hieratic, dehumanised Christ.

SYMBOLISM

Even when they illustrate some Biblical episode, the paintings with figures in the other buildings at Ravenna seem to have a symbolic value. Thus the baptism of Christ, the central scene in the domes of the two baptisteries, assumes at the same time the value of an epiphany, a proclamation of the Christ-God. The apostles who are looking on are there as well-known witnesses. Similarly, elsewhere, the prophets and martyrs, Magi and angels who transport us beyond our world set out on foot towards the celestial city. The lambs of S. Apollinare in Classe are shown leaving their fold as the saints leave the palace of Theodoric and the port of Classis on their way to Paradise. Paradise itself is sometimes depicted as a delightful garden, like that of the Shepherd of Hermas, or as a vision of Christ and the Virgin, guarded by angels, receiving the faithful like the emperor in his palace. At Galla Placidia the apocalyptic symbols of the four evangelists are grouped around the gemmed cross in the sky, the ox (Matthew), the eagle (Luke), the lion (Mark) and the man (John). And the Christ in the apse of S. Vitale is seated on the globe of the world.

It is this evocation of the higher world, enveloped in the

42. **The apse, St Apollinare in Classe.** 6th century. Ravenna. The charming landscape and sheep represent the scene of Paradise with St Apollinare adoring a cross in a starred medallion, flanked by the busts of Moses and Elias in an evocation of the Transfiguration. Above is Christ blessing, between the symbols of the Evangelists. The twelve sheep climbing towards him from the cities of Jerusalem and Bethlehem represent the saved souls of the faithful. To the right and left are the archangels Gabriel and Michael, and figures of saints appear between the windows.

blue of the sky and the gold of the sun, that is to be found in all these works—and gives the decoration its value. Prophets, saints, apostles, martyrs are everywhere proclaiming and acclaiming the divinity of Christ and the truth of his promise. In its symbols, as in its colours, the decoration of the Ravenna churches revives the hope of salvation. Some commentators have emphasised the serenity with which the catacomb paintings depicted the fate of sinners, where there are no devils, no sins, no judgement, no hell: we are far removed from terrifying Christs, leaping devils and the crowds of the damned cast into hell which

were soon to hold man in dread. They are equally absent in these sanctuaries intended for the living, which glitter like palaces and in which there is no shadow, no sadness and no penitence. The betrayal of Judas and Peter's denial are episodes in the past and have been fulfilled as was prophesied. Christ has come and occupies his royal place in the world where even emperors must serve him. Surrounded by his angels and saints, he awaits the faithful in Paradise. Even the Apocalypse becomes a promise and not a cause of fear. At Ravenna, one is really tempted to wonder whether there are any damned.

The Architecture of the Dome

43. **Hagia Sophia.** 532–537, Constantinople. Between the Turkish minarets the magnificent basilica, designed by Anthemius of Tralles and Isidorus of Miletus, is seen here from the front showing the half-domes either side of the central dome, and the supporting buttresses of the side arch.

THE PROBLEM OF THE DOME

Byzantine architecture was born from the introduction of the dome into the structure of the churches—a correct, if inadequate definition. After all, there were domed monuments before Justinian, some of them very large indeed, the Pantheon at Rome for example, which dates from the time of Augustus. There were even certain **Christian** sanctuaries which, as we have seen, adopted the form of the imperial mausoleum, the first being the rotunda built over Christ's tomb in Jerusalem. But the domes were still lids placed upon cylinders, on thick walls that had no difficulty in supporting their weight. The concrete vaults, invented by the Romans for their *thermae*, had been rounded into domes over *caldaria*, monolithic domes, which they later tried to lighten by mixing volcanic stone or even cylindrical pottery chains with the cement. The half-domes of the basilicas too had given the masons some training. Some of those in Syria were made of carved stone, but elsewhere they were usually made of more or less lightened concrete. It was easy as long as the supporting wall was round.

The real problem appeared when the dome had to be placed on a square base. This is still quite an easy matter when the monument is small, like those innumerable *marabouts*, or tombs of saints, covered with a dome, that add so much charm to Islamic landscapes. A stone placed across each corner of the square was enough to form an octagonal base on which the circular base of the dome could be placed. This overhanging stone may be replaced by an arch; link this arch to the corner by a piece of vaulting, and you have a squinch; and the dome supported by squinches was to have a long history both in the Christian art of Mesopotamia and in the Romanesque art of the West.

The difficulty increases, however, when the dome must be placed, not on a cube of walls, but on four great arches, like those of the *martyrion* of St Babylas at Antioch Kaoussié. These supported a pyramidal wooden roof. If one wishes to replace this roof by a dome, even the lightest possible one, one must first solve the problem of the thrusts. A dome does not just squash the pillars supporting it, but tends rather to force them outwards and collapse.

Byzantine Asia used brick as its building material. The Romans knew about bricks and used them for facing walls and for coursed work. They seldom used them in the building of whole walls or for supporting arches and never for domes. Brick is a cheap material, easy to make, lay and

44

31

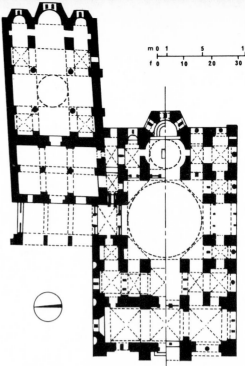

45. **Plan of Hosios Lukas.** *c.* 1040. Stiris, Greece. This typical example of a Byzantine church of cross-in-square plan shows how the central dome was borne by four separate supports forming a square. The three apses at the east end and the narthex are also characteristic features (see plate 70). The main church, the Katholikon, shows the transition from the square to the dome without interior support, by means of an octagon on squinches.

44. **The squinch.** This view of the 11th–century church of Sta Fosca, Torcello, clearly shows the use of two squinches, one placed above the other, to progress from the vertical walls of the arches to the round drum supporting the dome (in this case replaced by a circular timber roof).

align—and easy, by means of divergent cement joints, to form into an arch on a frame. The engineers of the 5th century had perfected the techniques of the barrel vault, the groined vault and, finally, the dome: so it became easy to make the covering joints that an architect's audacious ideas might necessitate. We know very little of the preparatory developments that led up to these technical exploits. The Byzantine masterpieces sprang up almost simultaneously in the first thirty years of the 6th century. They did not develop out of Roman architecture, nor from the ancient architecture of Mesopotamia, where bricks had been used to build extremely thick walls, but because of an innovation. This was the brilliant invention of the pendentive, replacing the squinch at the corners of the square intended to support the dome. The pendentive is a spherical triangle. It is a section of dome which starts at the corner of the square from the capital of the pillar and then rises between the two perpendicular arches until it reaches the top of them. The four pendentives meet forming a circle poised at the top of the canopy formed by the pillars and arches; this circle therefore rests at four points on the keystones of the arches and also on the successive courses of the pendentives. It is from this circle that the dome rises—whether directly or on a drum of the height desired; before long the drum was pierced with windows. The thrust of the dome is thus distributed over the whole *extrados*, or outer curve, of the arches and descends, through the arches and the pendentives, to the four pillars of the baldachin. So it is these pillars and arches that had to be reinforced in order to prevent them from splaying out. There were a limited number of solutions and it was from a combination of these solutions that the basic principles of Byzantine architecture were to emerge.

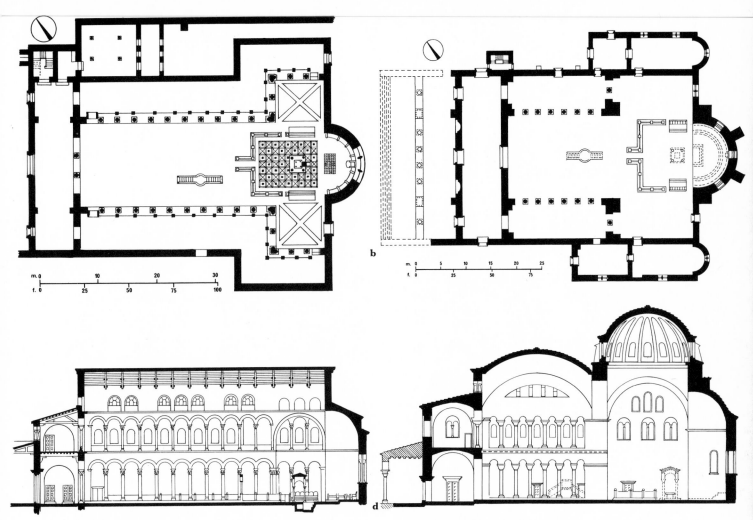

46a, b, c, d. **Philippi,** Macedonia. *(a)* The 5th-century church is a columned basilica with projecting apse and transept. *(b)* An analogous plan was reinterpreted in the 6th century, where the central dome and the thrusts imposed by it did not affect the basic basilical lay-out. *(c)* The colonnades of the 5th-century building carried a timber roof of limited height, while the dome of the 6th-century basilica *(d)* dominates the whole construction, giving it an entirely new majesty.

The first and simplest of these was to regard each pillar of the baldachin as the angle of two walls: there would thus be four naves, in the form of a cross, proceeding from the central square. Naturally, they would be vaulted: the walls would strengthen the piles and the vaults the arches, so controlling the thrusts of the dome. These vaulted naves could be replaced by apses, whose openings would merge into the arches of the dome and throw their weight on to the walls that supported them, and a vault could be placed between the arch and the apse. Lastly, the arches of the central dome could be juxtaposed with four secondary domes, of similar or different character, which would buttress the first. They, in turn, would have to be reinforced on the outside. We therefore have three schemes which automatically produce cruciform plans—either as a free cross, if the supporting elements are left separate, or as a cross inscribed within a square, if the basic structure is enclosed within four walls. In the latter case, there would be halls at each of the four corners, which could be connected to the large cruciform hall if necessary by openings of any size desired and whose vaults would contribute to the balance of the whole building. These theoretical schemes are in fact real plans, which were used in churches with the addition perhaps of an apse at the east end and a vestibule—a *narthex*—at the west.

It is equally possible, according to the sides of the square, to provide for different kinds of buttressing, which, both in plan and in elevation, would create dissymmetries. For example, there could be one apse and three barrel vaults, three apses and one barrel vault or one apse, two barrel vaults and a second dome.

These complex solutions were to be particularly popular on account of the pre-eminence originally accorded to the church of basilical plan. This plan consists of a rectangle, which has one dominant axis—and not four or even eight, as in a building based on the square. In order to extend this west-east axis, various subterfuges could be resorted to: simple additions—an apse at the east end, a longer nave at the west. But the structures themselves could also be adapted. Thus from apparently rigid technical principles several distinct schemes were developed, from which sprang some entirely original buildings. It is these exceptional buildings which usually represent Byzantine art in books: like all styles, it is represented by its masterpieces. But it is more useful, it seems, to look first at the plan that was used most commonly and which resulted from the normal application of basic principles.

A TYPICAL PLAN OF BYZANTINE CHURCHES

The plan of the inscribed cross, with central dome and internal buttressing vaults, was to become after the early period the typical plan of the Byzantine church and played the same role as the basilica with a nave and two aisles and a sloping roof in the previous period.

The dome is the centre as well as the summit of this type of building. It rests on the intersection of four naves which are of equal width and often very short. The end of the east nave opens on to a projecting apse. The cross is inscribed in a square, four halls adjoining the walls of the naves and the outside walls. These halls are more or less connected with the central cross depending on the number of openings between them. Their walls may be perforated by several doors, or may be replaced by arches resting on the pillars at the four corners of the central square. The adjacent halls are vaulted, in order to contribute to the buttressing of the building and the vaults play a more important role as the walls are opened up. They may be flat, and be concealed on the outside of the building beneath roofs with a single slope, or they may become domes—placed not on the arms of the cross, but between them—smaller domes which add to the loftiness of the central dome.

The churches of Greece, the Balkans and Russia are generally based on this type, sometimes treated on a large scale, and it was with certain variations the most common type in the 11th, 12th and 13th centuries and even beyond. Among the many examples in Constantinople is Zeirek Cami (Church of Christ Pantocrator) and in Greece, the smaller church at Hosios Lukas in Phocis, and the small *45* Metropolis in Athens. It is also found among the monastic churches of Mount Athos, and even as far away as Trebi-*80* zond in Sta Sophia.

When such a church has sufficiently light supports, and open arches, one finds oneself in a hall that looks almost basilical, with central nave and side aisles, whatever form the roofing may take. Sometimes one almost seems to be in a single hall, supported but not divided by columns, and ending in an apse.

THE BASILICAS AT PHILIPPI

The problem is different when the architect really wants to preserve a type of plan that has already been consecrated. A particular example will help us to understand both the profound change in structure which was brought about by new techniques and the imaginative effort which was now demanded of the engineer. Two basilicas have been discovered at Philippi in Macedonia, one of the 5th and the other of the 6th century. Their plans according to the works of P. Lemerle are very similar. It seems obvious that the client, that is the clergy, imposed on the second architect a ground plan that had been made necessary by

custom. But the very principles of building had changed—and in elevation the two buildings looked as different as could be.

We can leave to one side the outbuildings—the monumental courtyards which led up to the old basilica, the baptistery that continued its façade and the two absidal annexes flanking the main apse of the domed basilica. The two main buildings, including the *narthex*, were 185 feet and 182 feet long respectively. They were therefore of comparable size; but the façade of the older one was only 95 feet wide and at the transept 131 feet whereas the other had a uniform width of 108 feet.

The 5th-century church was a basilica with three aisles *46a,c* and galleries; it had a projecting transept, 46 feet wide on the inside, and a single detached apse. The colonnades continued around the transept, thus maintaining a side aisle of the same width: railings, fixed between the columns, seem to have forbidden the congregation access to the central nave as well as to the choir. The narthex, which also had a gallery, was covered by a sloping roof; the nave had a double sloping roof, which rose to 56 feet over a clerestory; the galleries of the side aisles had symmetrically sloping roofs. The building had some original features, but was constructed on the normal plan of its period.

The 6th-century basilica is based on the same scheme. *46b,d* It is a basilica with transept, but the arms do not project on the outside. It has the same narthex, the same apse and also the same liturgical arrangement in the choir: the synthronon, the altar placed between two side thrones, the chancels and the ambo are in almost identical positions. These are the liturgical requirements which had to be fulfilled in the first instance. But this time the intersection of nave and transept is surmounted by a dome, supported on pillars at either side of the apse and at the end of the colonnades of the nave. Buttressing behind the apse and the thicker walls in the angles of the side-aisles show a concern for greater stability.

The colonnades end at the pillars: they do not continue into the transept, so forming a large area of space, with high barrel vaults on the arms of the transept and the central dome, which reached a height of 110 feet. The intention is obvious: the apse and the arms of the transept controlled on three sides the thrust of the dome. One might have expected another simple solution on the west side of the central square; but here the obligation to maintain the basilical form arises—the need for side aisles separated from the central nave by a colonnade, the need too to preserve a gallery. At this point the architect had to make innovations and he regarded the whole of his central nave, the area within the columns, as a rectangular hall, which he covered by a groined vault 59 feet 6 inches wide and 85 feet high. It remained dominated by the main dome but helped to balance it, its own stability maintained by the superimposed vaults of the narthex and side aisles.

The comparison of the sections shows the complete *46c,d*

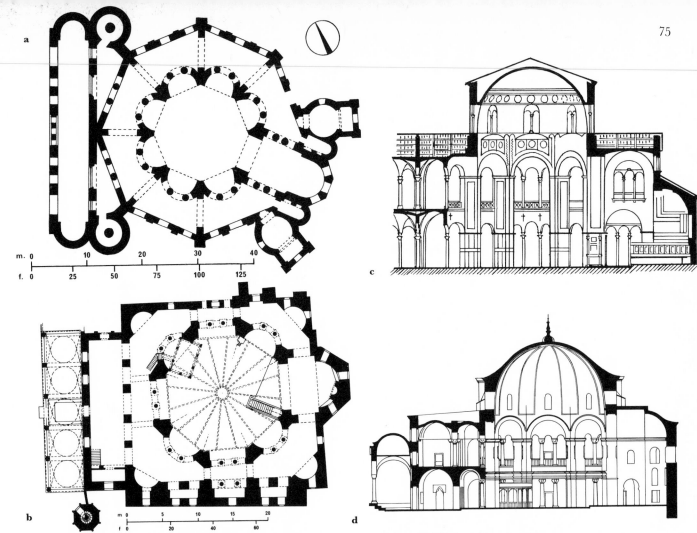

47a, b, c, d. **The plan of** (a) **S. Vitale,** Ravenna, is practically identical to the contemporary building of **H. Sergius and Bacchus** (b) (5th century). The sections show how the architect of S. Vitale (c) has given his monument an elegance and lightness in the height of the openings of the octagon not found in the church of H. Sergius and Bacchus (d).

contrast between the two buildings. The earlier basilica with its long, two-tiered colonnades must have been very pleasing, perhaps even majestic. But it had nothing comparable to the area of space obtained in the second building by the succession in the axis of the groined vault and the dome. This solution, which was so new and so successful, looks, all the same, like an expedient intended to solve a particular problem: fidelity to the traditional groundplan, which the clergy of Philippi demanded.

Justinian's architects were to use a similar method at the church of H. Irene in Constantinople. There were to be two successive domes, the first lower than the second and oval in shape. There was to be no transept, and the colonnades of the side aisles were to continue to the apse on either side of the main dome. It was another type of basilica which, by similar means, was reinterpreted in a new style.

SAN VITALE AND HAGIA SOPHIA

We are now sufficiently well equipped to study the plan of the masterpiece of Byzantine architecture, Hagia Sophia (Sta Sophia) in Constantinople. We must, in order to understand its structure, take a closer look at another building of the same period, S. Vitale, Ravenna.

S. Vitale, like H. Sergius and Bacchus in Constantinople, is a special case. In fact the dome is supported not by a square but by an octagon, marked by eight corner pillars, parallel to the outside walls, which carry eight lofty arches. These eight arches are in fact the openings of eight half-domes, which thus support the central dome. They in turn are not formed by solid walls, but by two tiers of very slender columns and very light arches, which give the whole structure a transparent, airy appearance. These half-domes are necessarily buttressed by vaults, on two tiers, which join them to the strong outside walls. In the circular side aisle thus formed, the placing of the columns is so complex that the whole plan seems to be hidden; and picturesque perspectives are created which add a quite unexpected charm to what is a purely logical structure. The difference between S. Vitale and H. Sergius and Bacchus shows how much the architect has gained by his accentuation of height and by replacing a horizontal moulding by arcades to support the gallery and by making his modules more slender. Even within a demanding and highly technical scheme individual talent can contribute something new.

The problem facing Anthemius of Tralles and Isidorus of Miletus, the architects of H. Sophia, was of a much greater order. The task that the Emperor Justinian had entrusted to them was of the greatest importance for him. During the Nika revolt which had followed his accession, several buildings constructed by Constantine in his new capital had been burnt down by the rioters and among

48. **Interior view of H. Sergius and Bacchus.**
Constantinople. 525. The robust arches of the interior of this
basilica give the impression of a vast area, but lack the
lightness and delicacy of the architecture of S. Vitale, Ravenna.

them were several churches, those of the Divine Wisdom
H. Sophia, and the Divine Peace, H. Irene. H. Sophia in
particular, was both the cathedral and the church of the
palace, which was situated between the church and the
hippodrome. It was imperative that the emperor should
declare his power and his glory with a monument that
would be more dazzling than any ever seen or heard of by
man. Legend has it that as he entered the finally completed cathedral he cried: 'Solomon, I have triumphed
over you.'

47 The technical problem that faced the builders was on a
similar scale. They had to raise a dome 75 feet in diameter
49b (the same size as the dome of the Pantheon in Rome) 75 feet
in the air and place it on four arches. This was to become
the summit of a series of vaults, which in all would cover
an area four or five times larger.

49a They decided to adopt a plan of simple symmetry. They
wanted to build a rectangular basilica, of which the length
would be twice its width. In the length therefore it was
sufficient to stabilise the dome by half-domes fitted between
the side arches and consequently having the same diameter
as the main dome. Each of these half-domes was buttressed
by three others, whereas at S. Vitale there are four. Two
of these were supported by two tiers of small columns.
The eastern one was closed to form the apse of the basilica.
At the west end, it was replaced by an internal porch. Thus
the main axis of the building was *c.* 250 feet long.

Now the arches on the left and right of the dome had to
be buttressed too. They were filled by a side wall of a
basilica, made of a row of five porphyry columns, bearing a
gallery with five more columns which supported a cornice
above bearing a semicircular wall pierced with windows.

This pierced wall, strong as it was, did not fully bear the **50**
thrusts of the huge dome, so enormous interior buttresses

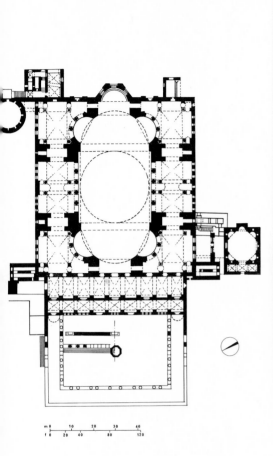

49a, b. **H. Sophia.** 532–537. Constantinople. Immediately
one can see in the plan the large area of space created by the
architects' decision to keep the dome in its principal axis
with two half-domes of the same diameter. (b) The main dome
was reconstructed in 588 by a nephew of Isidorus of Miletus
after an earthquake had destroyed the original, with its
flatter silhouette. It was built a third time after 989.

were placed against the wall behind the pillars. This was
merely static resistance, and when later the dome collapsed the weight had to be increased and continually so
throughout history. Superimposed groined vaults between
the sturdy arches covered the two-tiered side aisles.

As at S. Vitale the perspectives are wonderful with the
golden vaults appearing between the columns like sky
through trees. But the main impression is of the nave itself,
when, as one moves from the narthex through the central
door, one sees above the magnificent east apse, the main
dome brilliant with so many windows. One indeed wonders, with Paul the Silentiary, who gave the inaugurating
sermon, if it was not suspended from the skies by a golden
chain.

Unlike the cathedrals of the West this vast hall is not
apparently interrupted by bays, nor by side aisles, nor does
the amazing height of the vaults seem to detract from the
width. The side annexes seem to disappear. The width is
preserved completely all the way up the building, the
dome and two half-domes seem to push the walls apart
rather than bring them closer to each other. It is a single
space, undivided by the succession of curves in the upper
50 areas. As the light flooded into the splendid interior the
48 magnificent marble of the walls, the porphyry of the columns and the gold of the mosaics, enhanced its majesty.

THE EXTENT OF EARLY BYZANTINE INFLUENCE

Byzantine architecture began—or almost—with its masterpiece. Such buildings require means that are rarely at
the architects' disposal, but the principles which had been
worked out in such a masterly fashion at the beginning
were to be used for a long time afterwards. From the first
period, and within the realm of influence of Constantinople, there were to be a great many churches that show
an exceptional wealth of imagination.

It was during the Macedonian revival that, concurrently with the cross in square plan we have discussed before,
another type of building became common that had
previously appeared in Mesopotamia and which revived
the old technique of placing the dome on squinches. A
square hall was formed in which the dome was supported at
eight points instead of four, the arches of the squinches
transforming the square into an octagon above the main
arches. The development of the supports introduced between the central hall and the outside wall, which was also
square, a series of annexes of different forms.

Some of the best known churches of the Greek world are
of this type, including those that are famous for their
mosaic decoration, which will be discussed later.

It must not be imagined, however, that the building
methods adopted by the Byzantine architects were uni-

50. Interior of Hagia Sophia. 532–537. Constantinople. The soaring dome and spacious apse of the great Byzantine masterpiece seem poised on a succession of arches. The pendentives supporting the dome and the arcades and perforated wall of the side arches are clearly seen in this view. The Arab medallions date from the time the building was used as a mosque.

51. **The cathedral of Aght'amar.** 915–921. Lake Van, Armenia. The eastern façade of the church shows the original sculpted decoration, the foliated scrolls and figures in flat relief. Built for King Gagik by the architect Manuel it is a square plan buttressed by four apses, enclosed in the outline of a free cross.

versally accepted. They spread mainly through the Greek and Slav world. In the West, as we shall see, the power of Roman traditions, on the ecclesiastical as well as the artistic plane, moved Merovingian and Carolingian art in a quite different direction. Even in the East, the regions which had previously developed a particular architecture persisted in their own ways and by their resistance changed their models, although sometimes they were looking for new inspiration. The Syrian architecture of the 6th century develops within its own terms. Whether basilicas or buildings with centralized plans, the churches of Justinian's time proceed from local precedents. In the more magnificent churches, there was a tendency to replace the colonnades of the basilica with great arches placed on low pillars—as at Brad and Ruweha, but this had already been done at Qalb Louzeh in the second half of the previous century. Similarly, the projecting apses, the fantasy of the mouldings on the façades, the flat forms of carved foliage and the mosaics of flower seeds had been part of Syrian tradition for some fifty years. When a building was built by one of Justinian's architects or under their direct influence—such as the great dam of Antioch in the valley of the Parmenios, the chapel and palace of Qasr-ibn-Wardan on the edge of the desert, the cistern in the citadel of Aleppo, the trefoiled choir at Bethlehem—it seems foreign. At R'safah in the middle of the desert the pilgrimage town built around the tomb of St Sergius is perhaps the only example of a compromise.

In Egypt it is the same, and it is the author's belief that there was no distinct break between the buildings of the 5th and 6th centuries, or even those that the Copts continued to build after the Islamic conquest. They began as basilicas, sometimes with a transept, as in the pilgrimage church of St Menas near Alexandria, or again as at Sohag and in the monasteries of Wadi-Natroun, with an internal colonnade along the four walls, and a trefoiled sanctuary: a similar type from the 6th century is to be found at El Flousiyah (Ostracine).

ARMENIA

The monuments of Armenia are more complicated and richer as Arab occupation did not last as long and was less efficacious; the Byzantine influence was also more direct.

The Armenians are a wilful and independent race and yet they have rarely been able to maintain their independence on the high plateau they occupied to the north of Mesopotamia, between the Roman territories and Iran. Conquered in turn by the Romans, the Persians and the Arabs, they retained enough personality for the Iranians and Arabs to entrust the government of their Armenian provinces to members of the local aristocracy and for Armenians living in Constantinople to attain the highest positions of command in the armies and even in the empire itself. Leo V (813–20) is alone in being recognised as an Armenian by Byzantine historians, but Basil II, born in Macedonia, is rightly believed to have been of an Armenian

family, and Armenian families had been ruling in Constantinople for two hundred years. Two further proofs of their vigour are that under the Arab occupation the Armenians remained Christians and when the Byzantine domination, which had increased considerably during the 11th century, was beaten by the Seljuks at Manzikert in 1071, the Armenians crossed the Taurus and settled in Cilicia to escape from this new domination.

The evangelisation of Armenia took place at a very early date. It seems improbable that the first sermon was given in Armenia by one of the apostles; but as early as 301, King Tiridates was converted by St Gregory the Enlightener and made Christianity the State religion. So that as elsewhere in the 4th and 5th centuries basilicas with three naves were being built which, in their ground-plans, were very like those of Syria. But the Armenian architects had their own building methods, so much so that at this time most of their churches were vaulted—concrete vaults on stone walls with bonded surfaces but with ashlars cemented between the facings. The Armenian basilicas at Ereruyk and Tekor thus have a very marked character of their own and are decorated with elegant mouldings as in Syria.

In the 7th century Armenian architecture took a new departure: as in Byzantium it became from then on an architecture of the dome on a square ground-plan. This scheme, which had been that of the cathedral of Echmiadzin as early as the 5th century, resulted in the creation of astonishing forms. Building methods had not changed, brick was not yet used. Despite attempts to make the concrete lighter by mixing volcanic matter into the cement, concrete domes much heavier than those of the Byzantine churches were placed on stone walls. These were built very thick, with small openings for doorways, and many of the

52. **Cathedral at Mtskhet.** 10th century. Georgia. The plan of the cathedral is comparable to that of Ani, but in a more complex interpretation. The fine mouldings decorating the façade are also comparable to the Armenian church.

full-length figures, medallions and animals in flat relief, and by ox-heads and lion-heads in the round. The frontally placed saints and angels in their outline and the technique of the line engraving used in the costumes call to mind the transcription into another art of the Armenian paintings that are very close to Byzantine art, and traces of which have been preserved in this very same church. But the overall impression is entirely original and many of the details appear to derive from non-Byzantine traditions: the feet in profile as in Parthian art, for example, or a king crouching on the ground, as in Sassanian art, not to mention other characteristics which, as they also recur in Armenian miniatures, may be regarded as of national origin—with a special and delightful blend of realism and stylisation. This façade sculpture, which was quite foreign to Byzantium, accentuates the intensely individual quality of Armenian art.

GEORGIA

Georgian art encountered similar problems: the Caucasus region was also affected by political and cultural influences from Mesopotamia and Syria on the one hand and from Sassanian Iran on the other—it was Miriam, the son of a Persian king, Sapor I, who became king of Georgia and was converted in 323, who first brought Christianity to the country. However, until the 6th century, the Georgian Church was a branch of the Church of Antioch, and so had a double dependency.

Yet, like Armenia, Georgia developed an original architecture: it too used vaults, and for this reason preferred chapels with a single nave and, later, basilicas with aisles separated either by very thick wooden pillars or even by unbroken walls. Thus, at Bolnisi-Kapanachki, in the 5th and 6th centuries, triple churches resulted. There were also cases in which the three vaulted naves give on to a perpendicular narthex linking them together (Nikapari, Zegani—6th century). Other basilicas with great arcades are reminiscent of Syrian buildings.

Side by side with this there developed a domed architecture, based first of all on a centralised ground-plan. After the 10th century, the dome was adapted to the basilica with great arcades and in the 12th century this finally became the accepted type. The ties between the Georgian kings and Constantinople were then at their closest: the niece of Bagrat IV of Georgia had married the Basileus Isaac Comnenus. This no doubt explains how Byzantine schemes were introduced into Georgia, how they were immediately adapted to local building methods, and how plans created in Georgia passed into the West—which was helped by the building of Georgian monasteries on Mount Athos or in Jerusalem.

Such exchanges show the limitation of the Byzantine expansion which was total only as long as it did not encounter flourishing technical traditions in a particular area, where the new designs may have been accepted, but were then adapted in an original way.

ground-plans of the churches seem very compact, with apses that look like niches and narrow adjoining halls like corridors. But inside the buildings are strangely slender and outside the plan seems to be enclosed in cruciform areas, with roofs concealing the domes and vaults, thus producing the outline of a Greek church.

These slender, graceful stone buildings are decorated on the outside with very fine arcatures, which enhance the elevation even more. Sometimes a carved decoration is added which may be either geometrical with flat motifs as at Ani, or with light mouldings as at Ptghavank or with foliated scrolls enclosing animal figures. All these motifs are found in a church which is the oldest masterpiece (c. 915) of Christian carved decoration, at Aght'amar, on an island in Lake Van. Protruding from the stone walls, and running round the whole of the outside of a complicated cruciform building with octagonal dome and corner niches, this decoration is entirely without rules. There are a continuous cornice beneath the roof, a foliated scroll forming a frieze and rounded mouldings over the windows, but the remaining free space is overrun haphazardly by

Iconography

Christianity is a religion of the Book. In its two parts, the Old and New Testaments, the Christian Bible is primarily a book of history—the history of the Jewish people and the biography of Jesus. Certain chapters have a lyrical, liturgical or prophetic character—the Psalms, Deuteronomy, the Apocalypse. But on the whole the narrative character is dominant.

Was it for pedagogical reasons, or out of a profound need to portray the characters and events of the sacred text, that Christians turned so early to book illustration? There are a great many examples of Octateuchs or Gospel-books illustrated with miniatures. Apart from a few exceptions such as the magnificent purple manuscripts of the Vienna **97, 98** Genesis or the Gospels of Rossano, which are thought to date from the 4th century, the examples that have been preserved are not of very early periods, but generally of the 10th or 11th century. There is no doubt that they have a long tradition behind them. From generation to genera- **100** tion, the illuminations were recopied as well as the texts, not only in a spirit of imitation, or through lack of imagination, but because the pictures shared in the sacred, inviolable character of the book they illustrated—they constituted an iconography.

At the same time as the first miniaturists, the fresco-painters and mosaicists, seeking to glorify the main events of Christian history in the churches, were also working out representations, but of particular episodes. The arrangement of these separate images in the architecture sometimes **53** tended to form them too into cycles, and it is difficult to say which came first, the mosaicist or the miniaturist. It seems that in some cases the illustrations used for presenting particular scenes were simply borrowed from monumental art. At other times, on the contrary, it seems that the church painter, called upon to extend his repertoire of pictures, would take some illuminated manuscript as a model. There **55, 56** is a definite homogeneity between many representations, whatever the medium may be.

Gospel-books and Octateuchs were highly illustrated. Each paragraph, almost each verse, had its pictorial commentary. As in the 'strip cartoons' of the modern press, one can follow the story simply by following the miniatures; beside the text itself a few Greek words are often only a short commentary, giving little more than the names of the principal figures. The illustration is continuous.

We know little of the origin or of the early character of these series. In the 4th century, Greeks and Romans used two kind of books. There were still the *volumina*, those long papyrus rolls, that so many statues of Roman citizens are shown holding, and in which the text followed regularly from one column to the next. According to the fragments we have been able to collect, it seems that the illustration was then limited to the width of the columns and executed **54** by craftsmen rather than artists. The Joshua Roll, which is on parchment, is regarded by K. Weitzmann as a work of the 11th century—not as other scholars thought a later

53. **Crucifixion.** 10th century. MSS Grec. 74, fol 99. Bibliothèque Nationale, Paris. The scenes follow each other in a narrow band below the text, according to a fixed iconography, although the style has great personality.

copy of a primitive original. Because of the very form of the surface provided, the images follow one after the other without a break, in long bands like the decoration on Trajan's column. On later manuscripts scenes often present, within an upright framework, compositions which have been cut or regrouped in a way that seems to point to the existence of long prototypes.

But from the 4th century, manuscripts more frequently took the form of parchment books—or *codices*—in which the illustration is still placed in the columns, but where it might also be expanded to a full page. Now the miniatures became real pictures where painters of quality could exercise their skill.

Very often, from one manuscript to another, the same scheme is used in the representation of a given scene. In the episodes from the Gospels, which were illustrated every time their text was recopied, the resemblance is indisputable. In order to distinguish between particular affiliations of style, G. Millet, in his *Iconographie de l'Evangile*, often had to pay special attention to differences of detail.

In attempting to form an idea of the prototype from which the later manuscripts derive, the copies which have survived have been so reworked that it involves a great deal of analysis. Usually this analysis leads to the conclu- **57**

82

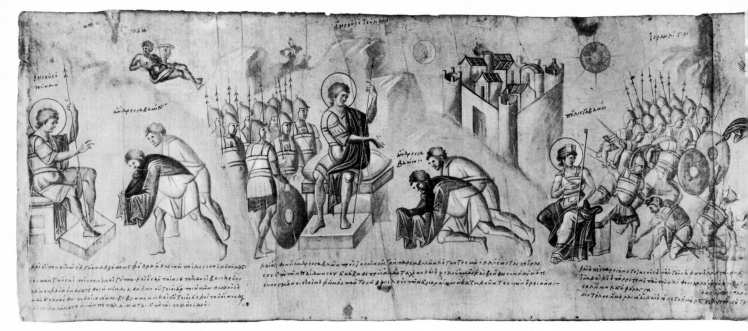

54. **The Joshua Roll.** 10th century. Vatican Library, Rome. This is an example of the illustration of text with juxtaposed pictures giving an impression of continuity. Here Joshua is seen in two scenes receiving the envoys from the town of Gibeon, who submitted to him and sought his aid against the King of Jerusalem and his allies. Note the personifications in the classical style.

55. **The Ascension.** 586. Miniature from the Rabula Gospels. Biblioteca Laurenziana, Florence. The monumental effect of the composition recalls the iconography of the ampullae from the Holy Land. The same arrangement is found throughout Western Christian art (see plate 115) except for the chariot of Ezekiel, here bearing Christ, heralding his second coming.

56. **The Ascension.** 15th century. 22½ × 15 in. (57 × 38 cm.). Hann Collection, Pennsylvania. Nine hundred years later the same composition is still used. Compare in particular the Apostles and the angels, and the stance of the Virgin Mary.

sion that at first there were only a small number of distinct models which even then had roots in common. And it must not be forgotten that in the case of the Old Testament the discovery of the cycle of paintings of the synagogue at Dura means that the possibility of Jewish models can no longer be excluded, perhaps even illustrated Hebrew Bibles in Mesopotamia.

However it must not be thought that this respect for the model deprived the painters of all opportunity to demonstrate their skill. The Octateuchs are full of delightful variations revealing the naturalism, the taste for the exotic, and the lively style of the different miniaturists. Although the artist had to be faithful to precedents he never followed them rigidly and there is consequently a great freedom of interpretation in the manuscripts. This is even more the case in large-scale paintings.

WALL-PAINTINGS

Byzantine painting was for a long time thought of as monotonous, stiff and so bright that it was in doubtful taste. Perhaps to distinguish its subtleties it should be studied more closely: today one can distinguish not only the different provincial schools, but also different stages of development. Of course one always begins at Constantinople and studies the development of art in the capital, then the influence of this development on the art of each province, thus realising its unity as well as its diversity.

Perhaps we should start our analysis by going right back to the beginning. Christian art was first experimenting when the empire, with the foundation of a new capital on the Bosphorus, was beginning to realise the fundamental importance of its eastern provinces. But these provinces were themselves being affected at this time by influences that came from farther east, from Mesopotamia and Sassanian Iran. This influence, which was to increase, is evident in certain of the late 4th-century mosaic pavements discovered at Antioch, but also in Coptic tapestries of the same period. The imperial art of Constantinople was sensitive to these innovations. It in its turn played a considerable part in the development of Christian art, which as a result was affected almost from its beginnings by an eastern influence, mingled with the Hellenistic traditions which flourished in both parts of the empire. We have already seen this at Ravenna, where the confrontation of models and styles from Rome and Constantinople is apparent in every building. Among the themes that Christian tradition was to hand down, there are bound to have been some that were originally treated in a Hellenistic style and others in an eastern style. But within a given motif, attempts could often be made to transcribe it from one style to another.

To be more precise, the Hellenistic style is spacious, light, supple and graceful, full of flowing figures which move in a three-dimensional world, achieved by *chiaroscuro* effects. The drawing creates living figures that are given depth and roundness by shaded colours. The clothes

57. **Night and the prayer of Isaiah.** 10th century. 14⅛ × 10¼ in. (36 × 26 cm.). The Paris Psalter (MSS Grec. 139), Bibliothèque Nationale, Paris. The classical personification of Night still has the costume, the floating veil and the attitude of Hellenistic painting as well as the technique, in this Byzantine psalter which was copied from an earlier manuscript (see plate 100).

are affected by wind and sun, the faces intended to express feeling and, in the backgrounds, the buildings assert their solidity and the trees are blown by the wind.

The 'eastern' style, on the other hand, tends to present the world in two dimensions. Space is abolished and replaced by backgrounds of a single, strong colour—deep blue or bright gold. When the background—buildings or landscapes—is not suppressed, it tends to be little more than indications of a scene with no perspective or illusion. Figures lose their bodies and become rows of frontal outlines. The treatment of the brocades is flat and mechanical and the folds a series of geometrical lines, replacing modelling with repeated coloured decoration or an abstract play of lines. The facial features are drawn strongly and symmetrically on to a flat surface where the huge eyes, wrapt in contemplation of the Beyond, glow with a supernatural splendour. We are in a magnificent and hieratic world, which evokes with certain fitting gestures, scenes that have been transported from the real world to that of the liturgy.

Of course these two tendencies intermingle, especially

58. **St Sergius.** 6th century. Mosaic. Church of St Demetrios, Salonika. The pillars of the church were decorated with ex-voto portraits of St Demetrios and other saints donated by the faithful. The mosaics are oriental in style, and strictly frontal, thus excluding all relief.

as Byzantine painting has recourse to at least four techniques. There is wax painting for the icons, usually portraits painted on fairly small pieces of wood; the miniature, used to illustrate parchment manuscripts, where the whole page illustrations sometimes resemble icons, and the complex scenes are sometimes related to those found in mural decoration, but treated on a very small scale; then there is mural mosaic, which is both monumental decoration and a figuration of characters and static or dramatic scenes; and, lastly, frescoes, which treat the same subjects, but with much greater flexibility.

Each technique has its limitations and its preferences. The mosaicist has neither the freedom of the fresco-painter, nor the opportunity to depict detail of the icon-painter. The miniaturist may choose either to draw freely on the parchment or to concentrate on the juxtaposition of brilliant colours. The subjects are the same, the manner in which they are to be represented is usually predetermined, but the mosaicist may, like the miniaturist or the icon-painter, place his figures against a gold background with greater ease than the fresco painter. Some of his success is at least partly due to the monumental aspect of his technique. The *Virgin* in the apse at Torcello, a slender **80** blue shape against a gold sky, owes much of its splendour to the material itself; and the *Pantocrator* at Daphni also **73** owes its overwhelmingly majestic effect to the material. Many icons and miniatures derive a magnificence from their gold backgrounds which is surprising in such small works, but which in no way detracts from the delicacy of the expression. But the mosaicists are almost unable to capture the vivacity and atmosphere which comes naturally to the fresco-painters and can be seen in some miniaturists.

Every artist must use his own technique, be guided by the qualities of his material and choose the effect he wishes to obtain with the means at his disposal. He may also abuse these means, or betray them. There are many mosaicists who try to conceal the fact that they are juxtaposing cubes and try to paint with cubes. There are also fresco-painters who covered their walls with false mosaics as if the choice of their method was simply connected with a desire for economy.

It might be thought that the difference in style which we are trying to establish coincides with a difference in technique, that the mosaic and the icon were naturally a more 'Eastern' form, the fresco and the miniature more 'Hellenistic'. An artist's personal taste is affected not necessarily by the choice of something which is easy, but by his school and period and by his own religious and artistic feelings, which he wishes to express.

This conflict, and alternation, this mixture of two stylistic trends is universal. It is only in recent years that it has been possible to realise this fully, when colour photographs have at last made it possible to make valid comparisons between works that are distant in location, but striking in the similarity of their schemes.

59. **The three Fathers of the Church.** 12th century. Mosaic. Cappella Palatina, Palermo, Sicily. St Gregory, St Basil and St John Chrysostom are represented in this 12th-century

Sicilian mosaic with the facial traits established by tradition (see St John Chrysostom, plate 69).

In this field value judgements are even more dangerously subjective than elsewhere. A critic who is sensitive to decorative art, and who tries to consider the works in the setting for which they were conceived, looking at them from the right distance and at the right angle, will have a natural preference for a vigorous, simplified yet subtle style that blends with the architecture. He will feel at ease **70,81** at Hosios Lukas, or even at Monreale. Whereas a critic who is attracted by atmosphere, and judges each composition on its own merits, absorbing the charm of the landscapes and the feelings expressed by the figures, will be delighted before the Hellenistic works—the frescoes in **85,86** Nerezi or Boiana where he will be influenced by aesthetic habits acquired through contact with the paintings of Pompeii of the Italian Renaissance.

When one turns the pages of a book on Byzantine painting, one is very struck by this interchange. The rows of **59** saints or angels and the static scenes of the emperor's coronation or of the Crucifixion alternate with the vast movements of the Transfiguration or the Descent into Limbo. A closer look shows the organisation of the monumental style taking over complex scenes, as in the Nativity in the Martorana at Palermo, or a tremor of life creep-

ing into the simplest compositions, even in a row of apostles, as in the Apocalypse at Karie Cami.

In the midst of so many works, spanning no less than seven hundred years, these observations help us to feel the similarities and the differences, to recognise on each occasion what derives from one tradition and what from the other, and to discern at what moment the artist's own personality, the expression of his own taste and of his own sensibility intervened.

ICONOCLASM

Thus in explaining any Byzantine painting first of all the iconography should be taken into account, then the duality of the painter's inspiration. Finally, an important historical fact must not be forgotten: for a hundred years figurative art was declared an anathema. This is what is known as the iconoclastic crisis.

Little artistic evidence of this crisis has been preserved. Once those in favour of images had returned to power, they destroyed not only the official texts of the iconoclastic emperors, but also the works of art that had been produced according to iconoclastic principles during the crisis. Such a decision could only come from the emperor: as far as we

60. **The Agony in the Garden.** 1295. Paint on plaster. Church of St Mary Peribleptos, Ochrid, Macedonia. The composition is traditional—showing Christ three times, twice in prayer in the presence of angels and the third time coming to wake the Apostles. The group of Apostles roused from their sleep is astonishingly varied and expressive. The fresco is signed by Michael and Eutychios.

61. **The destruction of the icons.** 11th century. Chludov psalter, State Historical Museum, Moscow. This psalter has 'marginal illustration', where the freely drawn miniatures are not in a frame. Here the crucifixion is depicted with two iconoclasts to the left smearing an icon of Christ with whitewash.

are concerned events begin with an intervention by Leo III the Isaurian, who, in 726, had the image of Christ on the front of the Bronze Gate of the imperial palace destroyed and replaced by a cross. The epigram inscribed beneath this cross explained that the Emperor could not bear to see Christ represented by an image that could neither breathe nor speak, and preferred a symbol. This struggle between the supporters of symbolism and those of anthropomorphism in images had already taken place in the Church. It recurred in this period with a violence it had never previously known, perhaps because of Jewish influence or, more probably, because of the example of the Muslims. Their reluctance to represent living beings in places of worship for fear of idolatry resulted in the creation of a decorative art, to which buildings like the Dome of the Rock, built by the Umayyad caliph Abd al-Malik in Jerusalem in 691, owe their extraordinary beauty. The iconoclastic edict of Yazid II in 721 had resulted in the wholesale destruction of images, including Christian symbols in the Christian churches of Palestine. And not all Christians, or even all bishops, were insensitive to the accusation of idolatry. Many felt inferior before such a search for purity, particularly it seems in the eastern provinces of Asia Minor, where the principal support for the Isaurian dynasty lay.

The crisis which, with its dramatic ups and downs, was to last for more than a hundred years caused the destruction of innumerable works of art, both in the churches and in other buildings. This explains the gaps in our information on eastern Christian art prior to the 9th century. The support given by the popes to those bishops who were in favour of images finally brought about a change in the policy of the Church Councils, which of course supported the decisions of the emperors. The main source of the conflict lay in the differences between the emperors and the various candidates for the succession. The final re-establishment of images, in 843, was the work of the wife of the iconoclastic Emperor Theophilus, the Empress Theodora, acting on behalf of her son, Michael III. It was marked by the restoration of the image of Christ on the palace gates. The crisis ended where it had begun: all that remained was to change once again the decoration of the churches, H. Sophia at Constantinople for example. And the event is still celebrated by the Eastern Church as a triumph of orthodoxy. The miniatures of the Chludov psalter make a 61 number of picturesque allusions to the events of this period.

This dramatic break and the disappearance of two series of works of art, did not interrupt the development of Byzantine art as much as one might have expected. One notices however a renewal of the relations between religious and imperial art, which until then had developed along their own paths, with occasional borrowings from each other but with no systematic blending of the two. But the post-iconoclastic sovereigns were to insist on the emperor's relations with Christ and his saints. The result was a whole series of images that clearly expressed the nature of a theocratic monarchy whose authority proceeded directly from the God who invested it, while the religious art itself seems to have returned to its old traditions.

The West

62. **Sarcophagus of Pyrenean marble.** 7th century.
Toulouse Museum. The existence of these workshops where
craftsmen continued to work the marble in motifs freely adapted
from classical art, shows the continuity of artistic pursuits in the
Merovingian period.

'MORE ANTIQUORUM'

Throughout the Roman empire—with the differences
which were created by the unequal spread of Christianity
throughout the provinces, architects and decorators were
faced with the same problems, which they approached
from the same fundamental principles. At the end of the
3rd century and during the 4th, imperial art did not vary
enough between regions to lead us to expect very deep
differences. There were the same basic concepts, the same
techniques and precedents: the variations of style to be
discovered, which are sometimes quite delightful, do not
detract from the religious and aesthetic unity of Christian
art.

It is therefore natural to find no fundamental contrasts
between Western and Eastern buildings. It was on a basis
of Roman art that Christian art developed in Gaul: the
sarcophagi of Provence are directly related to those of
Rome and the basilicas and baptisteries of the 4th century
were built according to universally accepted principles. It
is occasionally possible to find, apart from directly Roman
influences, a certain Syrian inspiration, perhaps in the
form of a baptistery or in the drawing of a foliated scroll.
This is because Christianity was first introduced among the
Gallo-Romans in the Syrian colonies of the Rhône valley.
But it is only a question of minor differences.

Gaul was later to prove more conservative than the East.
This was largely because of the impoverishment that was
to afflict the whole of the West as a result of successive
invasions. Insecurity is no more favourable to architecture
than the economic crises that are inevitably produced by

deep changes in the political system and in social relations.
And this was the case in the 5th and 6th centuries. However the Barbarian chiefs had shown an immediate desire
to build; for them this was undoubtedly a sign that they
had at last achieved stability and abandoned their nomadic
past. Even if they did not all manage to do what Theodoric,
who had been educated in Byzantium, realised at Ravenna,
they all wanted to have palaces and to provide their subjects, conquerors or conquered, with vast, elaborately
decorated churches. At Toulouse, the cathedral—the
Daurade—proclaims even in its name the splendour of its
gold ceilings, and at Auxerre and in Paris, the Gothic and
Frankish princes competed with each other. Clovis built a
basilica dedicated to the apostles which was later given
the name of Ste Geneviève; and Childebert, again in Paris,
built a church called Ste Croix at St Vincent and a cathedral dedicated to St Etienne.

The Lombards at Pavia, Monza or Como and the Saxons
in Kent or Northumbria made an effort comparable with
that of the Franks and Goths. But what models could their
builders have used? What were their traditions? Who were
they, and who their workers? It is quite obvious that at the
time when these nomadic tribes finally settled they had
neither architects nor masons. The buildings that have
been discovered in various parts of Germany, made of
wooden stakes and mud, could hardly have had a greater
influence than the tents of the Arab nomads in countries
where the Romans had introduced or developed a magnificent architecture of stone and concrete. The Barbarians
hastened into the empire probably because they had been

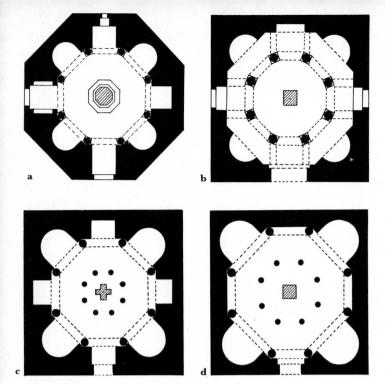

a   b   c   d

63a, b, c, d. **Plans of early Christian baptisteries**
5th century *(a)* Albenga had an octagonal plan with internal
niches, as was sometimes seen in the *caldaria* of Roman baths.
(b) Riez had a square ground-plan with corner niches and an
interior octagonal arcade. *(c)* Frejus is also a square plan
with alternate rectangular and horseshoe arched niches. *(d)*
Marseille was a square plan with an interior octagon and
corner niches and colonnades.

64. **Bronze decoration for a moneybag.** 7th century.
Found at Wingles (Pas de Calais, France). Musées Royaux d'Art
et d'Histoire, Brussels. In the angular motifs one can decipher
interlacing patterns and birdheads. The central piece is
composed of eight S-shaped animals intertwined round a cross.

driven out of their previous territories resulting from a
chain of upheavals in the depths of Asia; but they were also
drawn by the attraction of a legendary civilisation based on
agriculture and the city. They were seeking cultivated
land, which their tenants were to continue to work for
them, and houses to live in. The archaeological discoveries
made on the territories that they passed through show the
attraction that an object from the Roman empire had for
them—whether they had obtained it by barter, by
diplomatic exchange or by the looting of a foray. Once
they had settled, they set themselves up on the Romans'
lands, in their farms, in their houses and in their churches.
And they had new ones built by the conquered natives who
had changed neither their taste nor their traditional techniques. In Italy, Gaul, Spain and Africa, Roman architecture continued, in its provincial forms, sometimes
declining during times of battle and crisis, sometimes re-
discovering something of its former vigour when a chief
established his power and fortune.

If the migrants did not bring with them new architectural methods, at least they had developed, like the Celts
before them, their own techniques for the minor arts,
chasing and enamelling, which they may have borrowed
in part from the Persians or the Greeks of the Black Sea
while they were still in Asia or southern Russia. They had
their weapons and trappings, their drinking vessels and
jewellery, and probably also, though nothing remains of
them, their fabrics and carpets. They were all decorated in
the same style which seems to owe nothing to Mediterranean art. It is not representational but decorative, geometrical and stylised, sometimes covering the surface with
a linear pattern; sometimes introducing motifs recognisable as originating from plants like foliated scrolls, but it
has nothing of the realism, even in the most abstract transposition, of Greco-Roman art. Everything is subjected to
the complex rhythm, to the proliferation of curving lines;
and even when animals are introduced into the decorative
scheme they are forced to undergo all the transformations
the continuity of the pattern demands.   *64*

Such an art could pass from bronze to the velum of
manuscripts. It was more difficult to transmit on to stone
and few attempts were made to do so, except in the British
Isles. And in any case Christianity would have difficulty in
introducing its iconography into a graphic system that was
so foreign to all representation. It is thought that Daniel
among the lions can be recognised on a belt buckle found in *65*
Switzerland; but these lions are heraldic and the prophet

(Continued on page 105)

49 (opposite). **Interior of S. Lorenzo, Milan.** *c.* 370. The huge
quatrefoil structure of S. Lorenzo is of double shell design, the
interior being surrounded by ambulatories and galleries, as can
be seen in this view of the eastern apse. Although much has been
changed in later remodellings, the grandeur of the original plan
and construction gives an idea of the importance of Milan in
Early Christian architecture in the West.

50 (left). **St Ambrose.** 5th century. Mosaic. Church of St Ambrogio, Milan. The figure of the saint has a humanity which comes from classical art, in spite of the Oriental influence which explains the lack of relief. St Ambrose is numbered among the four great Latin doctors of the church; while still a catechumen in 374 he was elected by the people to the bishopric of Milan. His influence extended throughout the Christian world, not only by his teaching but in church architecture and matters of state.

51 (opposite, above). **Baptistery of St Jean.** 7th century. Poitiers, France. The elements of pre-Carolingian Frankish architecture can be seen here as in no other building above ground in France: supporting arches, blind arcades, and capitals of Pyrenean marble.

52 (opposite, below). **Tomb of Theodochilde.** 7th century. Crypt of St Paul, Abbey of Notre Dame at Jouarre, Seine et Marne, France. Theodochilde, the first Abbess, died in 662; her coffin is decorated with rows of scallop shells divided by bands of a finely lettered inscription.

53 (opposite). **Charlemagne's throne.**
9th century. Marble slabs. Aachen (Aix
la Chapelle), Germany. The throne is
situated in the tribune, or gallery, at the
west end of the octagonal palace chapel,
which was created to show the grandeur
of the Emperor of the West. Facing the
altar, the throne was used for imperial
coronations throughout the Middle Ages.

54 (above). **The Ark of the Covenant.**
799–818. Mosaic. Apse of the Oratory at
Germigny des Prés. One of the few
mosaics surviving from the time of
Charlemagne, there are traces of
Byzantine feeling, especially in the larger
angels, which may be a result of
Italian influence. The little oratory was
built by Theodulf, Bishop of Orléans and
Abbot of St Benoît sur Loire, one of the
most distinguished figures at
Charlemagne's court.

55 (opposite). **The journey to Bethlehem.** 10th century. Paint on plaster. Sta Maria in Castelseprio, North Italy. These frescoes seem to be the work of Greek painters from Constantinople, and they seem to belong to the art of the Macedonian renaissance. Nevertheless the Italians who discovered them date them from the 7th century. The graceful scenes cover the walls of a tiny chapel.

56 (above). **St Stephen before the High Priest.** 9th century. Paint on plaster. Crypt of the Church of St Germain at Auxerre, France. The frescoes from the small side chapel dedicated to St Stephen represent three scenes from the life of the saint. They have been compared to manuscripts but may be derivations of catacomb paintings or early mosaics in Rome.

57 (below). **The stoning of St Stephen** is the third scene in the side chapel at St Germain, Auxerre. The Deacon turns in prayer towards the hand of God as he is stoned by two Hebrews. The gate of Jerusalem is depicted to the left. The scene is full of movement and heralds Romanesque painting.

58 (left). **Book of Durrow.** 7th century. $9\frac{1}{2} \times 6\frac{1}{2}$ in. (24 × 16·5 cm.). Trinity College Library, Dublin. This spiral page (fo. 3v. Codex Durmachensis) shows how much this favourite motif of the Irish miniaturist can be interwoven and developed. Here the development is highly original and shows links with Celtic art in Ireland of the pre-Roman period.

59 (below). **Detail from the Book of Durrow.** 7th century. Trinity College Library, Dublin. The detail of elaborate interlacing pattern from a page full of similar decorative areas shows the intricate weaving of the forms with the animal heads and tails, and the glowing colours so distinctive of the Irish manuscripts.

60 (right). **Title page of the Book of Kells.** End of 8th, early 9th century. Trinity College Library, Dublin. The beginning of the Gospel of St Matthew: *Christi generatio* (fo. 34 r.) shows how unbounded was the graphic imagination and sense of colour of the artist. The letter takes up the whole page, enriched with carefully balanced whirls and patterns, each different from the next.

ᚺᚵᚢᚱᚬᚮ

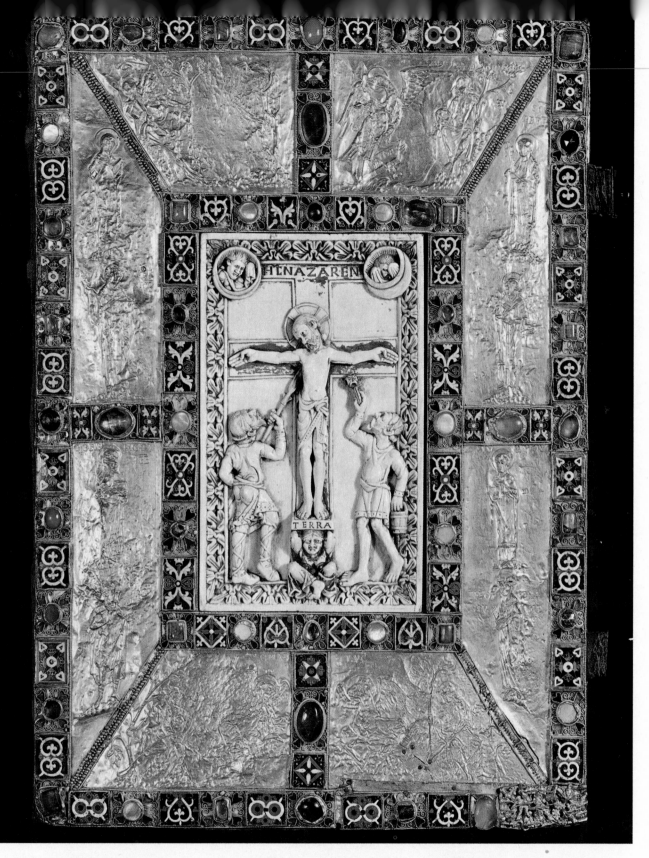

61 (opposite). **St Matthew.** End of 8th, early 9th century. 13 × 9½ in. (33 × 24 cm.). Book of Kells (fo. 28v), Trinity College Library, Dublin. The figure of the apostle seems to be standing, but is in fact seated in an armchair which blends with the decorative frame. In the same way the folds of the drapery form part of the design which is enlivened by the typical Irish interlacing pattern, and the animal forms spiralling round the border.

62 (above). **Cover of the Echternach Gospels.** *c.* 990. Ivory, beaten gold, enamel and precious stones. Germanisches Nationalmuseum, Nuremberg. The manuscripts of this and earlier periods (see figure 76) usually had covers of magnificent workmanship. The example shown was probably made on the orders of the dowager Queen Theophanu who is depicted below right. Her son Otto III faces her, and the other panels represent the symbols of the

Evangelists and several saints. The exquisitely carved ivory panel depicts the crucifixion, with the cross supported by the crouching figure of Earth, while above the sun and moon mourn the crucified Christ.

63 (above). **Christ Blessing.** *c.* 781. Bibliothèque Nationale, Paris. From an Evangelistary commissioned from the scribe Godescalc at the court school of Charlemagne. This page contains elements deriving from the early Roman Christian (see plate 12) and

Byzantine traditions, and the interlace pattern from Irish art.

64 (opposite). **St Mark the Evangelist.** Early 9th century. Gospel of St Médard of Soissons (fo. 180 v.). Palace School of Charlemagne. Bibliothèque Nationale,

Paris. This characteristic Carolingian manuscript was given to the monastery by Louis the Pious in 827. The motifs stem basically from Byzantine sources but they are interpreted in a very free style.

65 (opposite). **First Bible of Charles the Bald.** 851. Bibliothèque Nationale, Paris. The frontispiece of the 'Bible of Count Vivian' shows the Count, the lay Abbot of St Martin's of Tours (centre front), dedicating to King Charles the Bald, the grandson of Charlemagne, the Bible which is carried by the monks on the left. The solicitous and formal way in which the Bible is offered indicates the precious nature of the gift. The architectural details of the frame are typical of the classical tendencies at Tours.

66, 67. **The Pepin Reliquary.** 9th century. Gold, enamel and precious stones. *c.* $7\frac{1}{4} \times 7\frac{1}{4} \times 3\frac{1}{2}$ in. (18·5 × 18·6 × 8·8 cm.). Abbey treasury, Conques, France. The reliquary was given to the abbey by Pepin of Aquitaine (817–38). It is a small wooden casket covered with beaten gold plaques and filigree work and set with gems and cloisonné enamels. On the front (above) is the *Crucifixion*, with Christ in the centre on a cross edged with pearls. Either side are the Virgin and St John and on the slope of the lid are the sun and moon, usually part of the iconography of medieval crucifixions. The other side of the casket (below) has two eagles on the lid with brilliant translucent enamel wings. The top of the central filigree panel of the lid is set with an intaglio cornelian. This work shows little sign of Byzantine influence; it belongs strictly to the West.

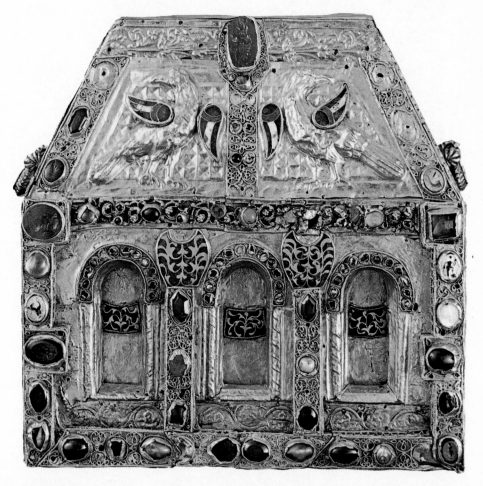

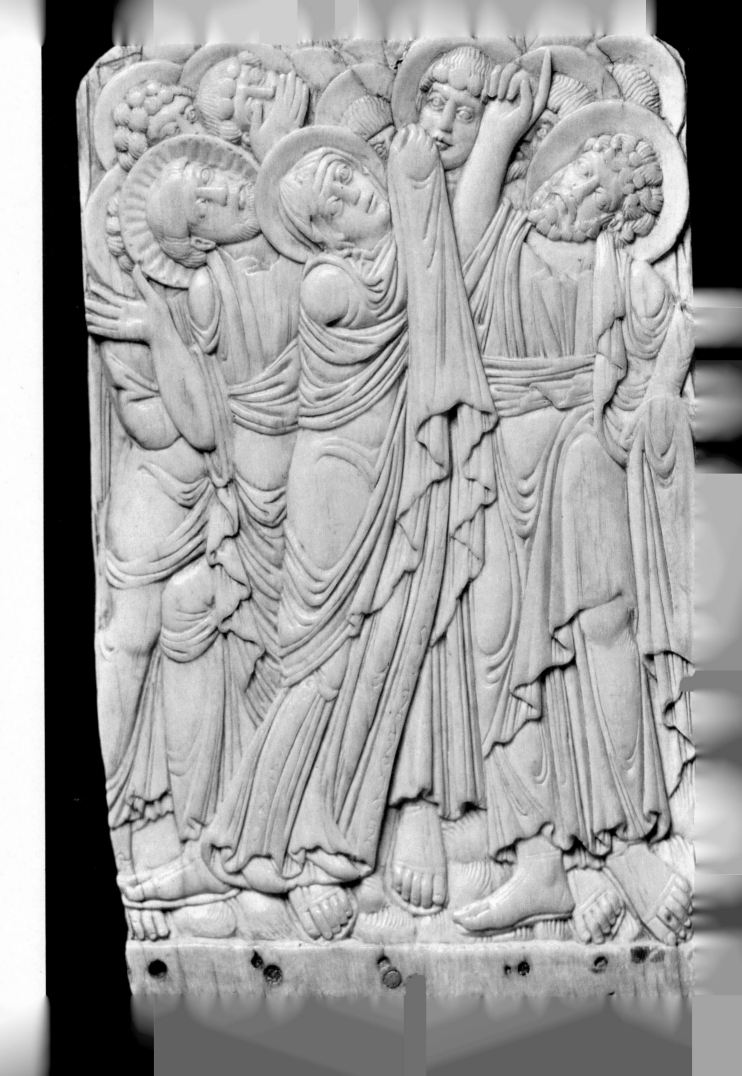

himself is rigidly stylised—much closer to the *Gilgamesh* of the Mesopotamian seals than to the prophet of the catacombs. In fact, throughout the whole of this period architects and masons claimed to be continuing to obey the Vitruvian rules: they worked '*more antiquorum*', or 'in the manner of the ancients'.

One proof of the activity of the builders, apart from the texts, is that there were workshops in the Pyrenees where marble was quarried and sarcophagi, columns and capitals were made which, with the re-opening of the ways of communication, spread throughout Gaul. The capitals, which are based on Corinthian models, are often charming in their originality and exquisitely carved. But even when they depart from the ancient canons, the acanthus leaves still curve away from the *calathos* with great suppleness to support projecting scrolls at the corners of the abacus. In the ancient manner they are surmounted by parts of an architrave: but they develop along their own lines quite differently from those followed by the Byzantine marble-masons—reducing the flat, pointed acanthus-leaves to an alternation of black and white triangles.

51 A building like the baptistery of St Jean, Poitiers, one of the few surviving examples from this period, with its interior decoration of blind arcades completing the line of the supporting arches, has a style very much its own which is accentuated by the solid Pyrenean capitals and the heavy mouldings they support. In the crypt at Jouarre, which was probably profoundly altered in character by a Romanesque rebuilding of the vaults, there are Pyrenean columns and capitals, sometimes almost classical in style, at others delightfully original. They surround some very different **52** sarcophagi, among which that of Abbess Theodochilde (662) derives its sober decoration from a double row of shells, separated by bands of writing which are decorative in themselves.

The transition is not abrupt from these buildings to **66** those of the next period—the crypt of St Laurent at Grenoble (8th century) or the oratory of Germigny des Prés, built by a bishop of Charlemagne's time. Even if little is known about the basilicas of the 7th century, or, for that matter, of the 8th or 9th centuries they were definitely firmly attached to Roman traditions. At St Denis, the monastery church, where the tomb of the apostle of Gaul was situated, was built in the Merovingian period, and restyled by Abbot Fulrad under Pepin the Short. Before being completed by Charlemagne in 775, it had a plan based on that of St Peter's, Rome, a basilica with a nave and two aisles, a transept and a projecting apse. The chapel

68 (opposite). **The Ascension** (fragment). Early 9th century. Ivory. $5\frac{1}{2} \times 3\frac{1}{2}$ in. (14 × 9.3 cm.). Landesmuseum, Darmstadt. This ivory fragment from a triptych was probably executed in the court workshop of Charlemagne. The Virgin and apostles form a close-knit group reaching heavenwards. Christ was doubtless represented on another panel borne aloft by angels. The intense movement and grace of the work transforms the Byzantine scheme.

65. **Daniel and the lions.** 7th century. Bronze. Length $\frac{1}{2}$ in. (10 cm.). Fribourg museum, Switzerland. This belt buckle found in a tomb at Tronche-Belon, near Fribourg, is an adaptation of the art of the migratory peoples to a Christian motif. Both the technique and the stylisation of the theme are characteristic.

66. **The Crypt of St Laurent, Grenoble.** 8th century. Grenoble, France. This vaulted quatrefoil building is decorated with blind arcades and small columns carrying Pyrenean capitals.

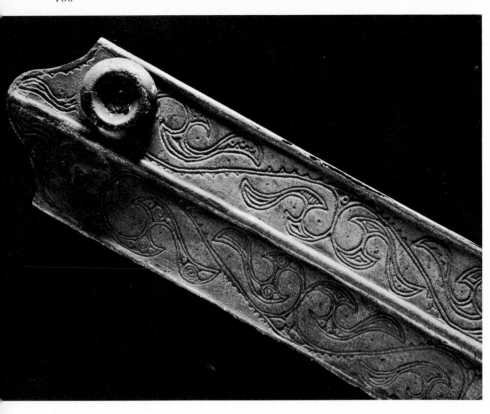

of the abbey of Fulda has a similar plan, but with a counter-apse, and the shrine of St Boniface, the apostle of the Germans, played the same national role. The introduction of monasticism by St Martin in the 5th century was to create a demand for more complicated schemes, which were to be treated according to traditional methods.

As far as this architecture is concerned, it does not seem that the 'Carolingian Renaissance' represented a new departure, but rather a flowering of traditions.

'INSULAR' ART

In the 7th century the art of the British Isles was to bring a new repertoire of forms and a new concept of decoration to the whole of western Europe, which was to reach its zenith in the illumination of manuscripts which had the greatest influence abroad. St Columba, born in Ireland in *c* 521, was the founder of a Christian movement of great spiritual intensity. He grouped his disciples in monasteries or hermitages, consisting of a cluster of huts around a poor chapel, at Derry and at Durrow, and tried to extend their knowledge as well as deepen their piety. He copied manuscripts himself—and one of those that have survived is probably his work, the Cathach, a fragment of a psalter, written in an archaic Irish form of capital letters.

69a, b, c

St Columba created other monasteries in Ireland before settling in Iona, an island off the coast of a part of Scotland that had been colonised by the Irish in the 5th century. This seems to have been the result of a desire to break with everything he held dear, and the Irish monks were to continue in the same spirit, emigrating in groups to distant and often desolate parts. In 590 a monk called Columban from the abbey at Bangor set out with twelve companions for Gaul and finally settled at Luxeuil, in the Vosges. After many attempts, and after leaving in Switzerland one of his disciples, Gall (whose tomb was to be the site of the famous abbey), he settled south of Milan, at Bobbio, where he died in 615. Shortly afterwards, another of his disciples, St Aidan, was to set out from Iona and settle at Lindisfarne, to the north of Northumbria on the east coast, and found communities as far south as Essex.

Irish monasticism thus seems to have spread rapidly across western Europe. It had its own particularly severe rules, and theological tendencies of its own which were regarded by Roman Christendom as archaic and were to lead to various conflicts. It represented a considerable intellectual achievement; Latin as well as Irish manuscripts were copied and among the monks there were poets, historians and chroniclers. They soon began to write the lives of their saints—beginning with St Columba.

These Irishmen were to tackle the conversion of Saxon England from their base at Lindisfarne. They then met with competition from missionaries sent from Rome. First, in the 6th century, Augustine who had been sent by Gregory the Great and had settled at Canterbury, then, in the 7th century an Asiatic, Theodorus of Tarsus, introduced Mediterranean culture to Britain. To them we owe the building of the first stone churches in England and, with the second mission, a whole flowering of Roman art, unparalleled in the Germanic world, or even, at that time, in the Frankish kingdom. It was particularly apparent in the decoration of certain stone crosses, and in the copying of Italian-inspired manuscripts, such as the Codex Amiatinus. 70

The conflict between the two missions, which came to a head over the fixing of the date of Easter, was to end with the victory of the Roman organisation. But the evangelistic activity of the Irish monks was to lose neither its strength, nor its originality. Thus in 678 Wilfred of York undertook

the conversion of Friesland and was followed by Willibrord who founded the abbey of Echternach in Luxemburg. And it was from Friesland that Wynfrith Boniface set out as the papal legate to convert the Germans.

In Great Britain at the end of the 8th century, the Viking invasions had forced the monks to abandon first Lindisfarne, then Iona, and after terrible massacres, the order retreated to Kells; but the Irish monasteries themselves were soon to be threatened and destroyed one after another.

This monastic movement had diffused over western Europe an art of the highest quality and one which is quite unlike any other. Its origin is a matter of dispute. It would seem natural enough that Irish monks should have taken with them an Irish art. Certain scholars, however, have tried to show that the first manuscripts to originate from Ireland—the first being St Columba's Cathach—are not highly decorated. There are only a few initial capital *69a, b, c* letters, which lead to quite simple graphic developments. They believe that the austerity of the saint was opposed to the luxury of decoration as he was to any other form of luxury and that it was only at Lindisfarne, when they came into contact with the art introduced by the Roman mission into Northumbria, that the Irish and their Northumbrian disciples returned to Celtic themes in order to oppose one art with another.

It is certain that this 'insular' art (using the term intentionally in order to avoid controversy) is connected, despite a long gap, with primitive Celtic art. Various attempts have been made to close the gap. Nils Aberg and Françoise Henry have enumerated sculptures or religious objects made of gold, which have been found in Ireland and which are of the 7th, 6th or even 5th century—and whose motifs form part of the decorative vocabulary of the weapons and jewels of the La Tène period, that is, prior to the arrival of the Romans on the northern coast of the Channel. These include the Battersea shield, or the scabbards found at Lisnacroghera Grannog. The spirals with which these are *67* decorated are also to be found on the Arkakillen Grannog brooch or on the very fine Ardagh chalice of the 8th cen- *68* tury. Curiously combined with others related to Coptic art, these motifs form the very basis of 'insular' illumination. It seems remarkable that they are already to be found in an embryonic form around certain of the initials in the Cathach. What is most striking in the more deco- *69a, b, c* rated manuscripts is that, in spite of allusions to the Christian art of Egypt, there is an absence of the Roman tradition itself. This was an art conceived outside the influence of the Romanised communities of Great Britain, and it decorates a great many manuscripts written in Irish; and even if it did not originate entirely in Ireland, it was the art of Irish monasticism.

IRISH MANUSCRIPTS

This art is made up of geometrical elements and non-figurative themes—geometrical decoration did exist in the Mediterranean art of both the Roman and the Christian periods, but it was a decoration which might frame figures, scenes or be part of a floor mosaic. It was never treated for its own sake. In 'insular' art, on the other hand, the motif dominates a whole page: as proof of this, one has only to look at the first page of the Book of Durrow, which is of an

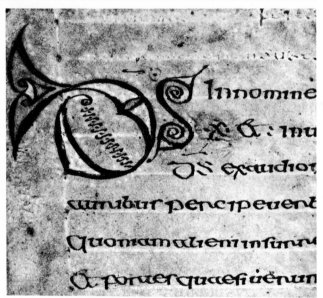

69a, b, c. **Initials from the Catach of St Columba.**
6th century. Royal Irish Academy, Ireland. The initials of
this manuscript are of a magnificent graphic quality. They
come from Celtic traditions and herald the Irish miniatures.

70. **The Bewcastle Cross.** 7th–8th centuries. The fusion of
barbaric ornament figure subjects and the vine scroll theme can
be seen in this early Northumbrian cross. Similar motifs are
found in the Irish manuscripts.

71. **St Matthew.** 7th century. 9½ × 6½ in.
(24 × 16·5 cm.). Trinity College Library, Dublin. The
strapwork can be seen again in this page from the Book of
Durrow, and the simplified symbol of the Evangelist is
decorated with a mosaic-type pattern also found in some of the
carpet-pages of this manuscript (see plates 58, 59).

72. **The four Evangelists.** End of the 8th century.
12 × 9½ in. (32 × 24 cm.). Book of Kells. Trinity
College Library, Dublin. The symbols of the Evangelists are
treated like heraldic motifs in a completely free graphic
interpretation. The frame is divided into bands allowing for a
variation of spiral and interlacing patterns. The patterns are
not always exact repeats.

elaborate intricacy quite foreign to Mediterranean art.
The almost total suppression of the straight line and right-
angle within the motifs gives the strips and borders the appearance of ribbons which tend to invade the whole of the
available space. This can be seen at once in the large
initials.

Quite naturally, when motifs taken from the animal
world are introduced into this decoration, they seem to be
taken up in the general movement. As we have seen, such
tendencies existed in the art of the migrant peoples; they
had also appeared in Italian initials. In a page of the Book
58,59 of Durrow, one can scarcely recognise the heads at the ends
of the volutes or the paws at the beginning. And even the
human face, so unexpressive, so enclosed within its frame,
71 that symbolises St Matthew in the Durrow Gospel-book,
was to be taken up in the movement of pattern in the Book
60,61 of Kells. Not only is there a rejection of space, but graphic
72 design replaces external form.

One should also emphasise that these manuscript pages,
though all dominated by these volutes, are in fact extremely varied. The form of the initial capitals, the importance

given to the lines of writing, the frames that suddenly
break across the decoration, the sometimes symmetrical,
sometimes spontaneous forms of the decoration, the magnificence of the colours, which are both rich and arbitrary
as in enamels, all this contributes to an impression of exu-
berant imagination—somewhat too vertiginous for a Mediterranean head. This art of Ireland, which only fifty years
ago was dismissed as the work of barbarians is now appreciated as an astonishing expression of the Christian faith.

THE CAROLINGIAN RENAISSANCE

The Carolingian Renaissance is no longer regarded as a
sudden illumination that came about through Charlemagne's own intelligence and authority. Yet it was a tempting idea to attribute to the Frankish emperor a role in the
West comparable to that of Constantine or Justinian.
Charlemagne had gone to Ravenna in 786 and to Rome in
800, and was thinking of precedents such as Rome, Byzantium and Ravenna when he decided to create a permanent
residence for himself at Aachen, a small watering place in
agricultural country. He was surrounded by Germans who

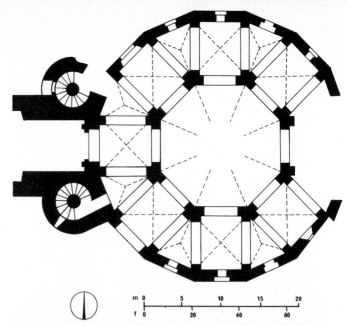

73a, b, c. **The Palace Chapel,** Aachen. Late 8th century.
(a) The interior view of the cathedral at Aachen shows the three-storeyed arrangement of the arches of the central octagon, seen in plan in *(b)*. The model *(c)* shows the exterior of the church.

always occupied the posts of military command or, like Eginhard, were in charge of the administration, but there were also foreigners. Alcuin, born in Yorkshire in 786, had acquired such a reputation for his knowledge that the emperor invited him to Aachen and entrusted to him the task of reviving art and the sciences. His role in the organisation of the schools, the Academy and the palace chapel, where manuscripts were copied, was of crucial importance; and through his impetus 'insular' artistic influences were kept alive in the court. They remained strangely subordinate, because at Aachen there were also Provençals, Lombards, Romans, Sicilian Greeks and Byzantine Greeks—not to mention Jews and Arabs. In this cosmopolitan court, to which the monarch entrusted the care of culture, art and education, certain men were given the task of transcribing the sacred and liturgical texts into a new style of writing, Carolingian minuscule, and of illustrating them. There were goldsmiths and builders—and all the different traditions had to merge together.

53 Quite apart from its own beauty, the palace chapel at Aachen is especially important because of the problem of the origin of its plan. It is a very high octagon, with an *73a* ambulatory. Because of its octagonal plan and also because of superimposed columns, it reminds one of S. *39* Vitale at Ravenna. But one must look closer. The plan is *73b* basically simple and like its large-stoned construction, it is Roman. What is particularly striking is the sturdiness, space and height of the interior octagon—and not the

clever articulation of a complex and subtle pillared building. It is a question of strength, not lightness: overhead, the arches have a short span, the capitals look Roman and are surmounted not by a Byzantine *impost*—a very characteristic pyramidal cushion—but by parts of an architrave in the Roman style. The interplay of the vaults looks like a series of improvisations, particularly the plunging barrel vaults of the gallery. On a basis of Roman traditions, with perhaps some idea of Byzantine compartmentation, the architect had to invent his own formulas whenever his experience did not provide him with a solution. And he liked to give his building a considerable height, which is somewhat concealed on the outside by the gallery roof *73c* broadening out beneath the lantern, but which looks surprisingly majestic on the inside.

It is rather of S. Lorenzo at Milan—and of the more **49** strictly western developments of the Christian architecture of the 4th century—than of the Ravenna churches that the palace chapel at Aachen reminds the author. There too one finds space and a certain majestic austerity, which are due to the height, to the sturdiness of the bonding, and to the decorative rather than constructional character of the interior colonnade. At Aachen there is no definite exterior support, but an original development based on traditional forms that were well known in the West. We have only to think of the Dome of the Rock, built in Jerusalem in 691 by caliph Abd al-Malik, and based on a similar plan that had been borrowed from that of the church of the Ascension on *16*

74. The Entry Pavilion to the monastery at Lorsch.
c. 830. Germany. This delightful decoration is composed
of a series of colonnades one on top of the other, and
polychrome facing.

75. The Tower of Earl's Barton Parish Church.
10th century. Northamptonshire. This is an unusual type of
decoration, with the local traditions interpreting Carolingian
art in an original way.

the Mount of Olives, to feel the gulf that separated the two
worlds—the difference between a kiosk—all airiness, colour and light—and this tall, ambitious, sombre tower.

In no other Carolingian building is the same audacity
to be found; but their architects were to show the same
mastery. Jean Hubert worked out the simple geometrical
rules on which their work is based: the equilateral triangle.
Charlemagne's palace at Aachen, or monasteries like St
Gall (820) or St Riquier (890) provided opportunities for
vast, ordered architectural conceptions, in which there
was scope to develop new forms and techniques. When
models were required, they turned to Rome. After the great
church of the abbey at Fulda, the plan of St Peter's in Rome
lost nothing of its prestige. It reappears, with variations, at
Hersfeld (980), Tours (995) and St Remi at Rheims
(1000). The buildings of the 9th and 10th centuries that
have survived are certainly very different from each other.
The astonishing façade of the abbey of Corvey, in Germany
(822), slender, flat, enlivened by its towers and high,
narrow veneered galleries; the exquisite polychrome façade
of the monastery portal at Lorsch (early 8th century); the
square tower of Earl's Barton, with its decoration of angular arches—these examples show that as far as elevations
and façades were concerned there were architects with
vigorous imaginations and their work can be seen reflected
in buildings in Vignory in Champagne and at Tarrasa or
at Oviedo in Spain.

74
75

WALL-PAINTINGS AND MOSAICS
Western buildings of the 5th century, like those of the 9th,
had been decorated in colour—by frescoes and mosaics.
Unfortunately, these have suffered even more than the
buildings and the few authenticated fragments which have
survived in each province are all the more valuable. One
notices with some surprise that these belong to different
traditions, so much so that it is sometimes difficult to believe that they belong to the same period. In Italy, of
course, the Roman tradition was still dominant. Its iconographical tendencies and pictorial technique may be
derived from the mosaics of Sta Maria Maggiore, which
date from 432–40. These tendencies and techniques re-
appear later, about 470, at Milan, in the chapels attached
to S. Lorenzo or S. Ambrogio. A taste for movement, for
large numbers of figures and complicated scenes give these
pictures a certain amusing, almost popular vitality. The
individual figures have lost their weight and relief, but contrary to what often happens in Byzantine art there is in
their attitudes and facial features a freedom of expression that gives them personality. These tendencies remain
dominant from the 6th to the 8th centuries in small Roman
sanctuaries.

Yet, in a little 9th-century chapel, at Castelseprio in
Lombardy, one finds frescoes that are truly Byzantine.
They show great charm in the way in which they bring to
life, through colour, the characters of iconographical

22, 23
24, 25
49, 50
55

76. **Christ and the Symbols of the Evangelists.** 7th century.
The Echternach gospels, (Cod. 61, fo. IV.) Cathedral Treasury,
Trier, Germany. The strapwork motifs of Irish manuscripts
are evident in this miniature from the famous 7th-century
Gospel book brought to the abbey at Echternach by monks
from Ireland. The symbols are painted in a stylised and
simplified manner.

77. **St Matthew.** 750. 15 × 12 in. (*c.* 39 × 32 cm.).
Codex Aureus (Gospel) fo. 9v, Kungl-Biblioteka Stockholm.
This miniature is a masterpiece of Anglo-Saxon monastic art
of classical inspiration. In other pages from the manuscript,
painted in Canterbury, there is an array of strapwork of a
typically 'insular' style.

tradition. They may have been painted by a westerner, but
certainly by someone who had been taught directly in the
East. Byzantine influences are also to be found at Cividale;
but further north, between Milan and the Tyrol, once
again one meets Roman traditions: the astonishing cycle
that covers the walls of the chapel at Mustair, in the Gris-
ons, with a series of Old and New Testament scenes and a
Last Judgement, retains the appearance of a Western work
both in its colouring (pink and ochre) and in its scenic
composition. The two decorations at Mustair and at
Castelseprio are almost contemporary and date from
immediately after the 'Carolingian Renaissance'.

Among the works produced by this renaissance one finds
the same disparities, either from one region to another, or,
within a particular region, from one building to another.
As in the East, there was a trend of hostility to icons among
the Frankish clergy of the 8th and 9th centuries which
resulted in architectural decoration, at Lorsch in Germany
and at Oviedo in Spain, for example, in which walls were
divided into geometric panels, or painted with scenes of
fantastic architecture. Behind these works was the strong
Roman tradition of carved marble mural decoration.

Elsewhere mosaics remain figurative: in the dome of the
chapel at Aachen the old men of the Apocalypse walk in
procession around the triumphant Christ—a motif created
in the 4th century in S. Paolo fuori le Mura, in Rome. At
Germigny des Prés, not far from his abbey of St Benoît **54**
sur Loire, Théodulf, the Bishop of Orléans, and a friend
of Charlemagne, chose a complicated decoration in a classical tradition. We know from the texts that it depicted
personifications of the seven liberal arts and the four
seasons. There remain only a few fragments of floral
decoration—palms and foliated scrolls—that seem to have
been affected by Islamic influences, perhaps from the
Ummayad palaces in Spain. There are also two winged
angels over an arch decorated with cherubim. The whole
group was perhaps intended to represent paradise.

The frescoes of St Germain d'Auxerre depict in an
astonishingly animated way the Stoning of St Stephen and **56, 57**
other scenes taken from the Acts of the Apostles. There
were also standing figures placed on pedestals, of bishops
and popes. On the one hand, we are in the midst of Roman
traditions and, on the other in contact with Carolingian
miniature painting.

(Continued on page 129)

69 (opposite). **The Emperor Nicephorus III Botaniates.**
c. 1078. (MS. Coislin 79. fo. 2 v.) Bibliothèque Nationale, Paris.
The miniature is from a famous manuscript of the Homilies of
St John Chrysostom. The Emperor is shown standing between
St John and the Archangel Michael. The glittering
costumes and rather flat pattern of the imperial figure can be
compared to the mosaic panel of Zoe and Constantine in H.
Sophia (figure 78), they are official portraits. The attitudes
of the figures and the excellence of the execution witness the
supremacy of the court workshops and the definitive influence
that their products had in the Byzantine empire.

70. **Hosios Lukas.** 11th century. Phocis,
Greece. The Katholikon (left) was built
c. 1020, and the Theotokos (right) *c.* 1040.
These magnificent churches of the
monastery of Hosios Lukas (St Luke in
Stiris) look out over a wide undulating
valley to the south of the road from
Athens to Delphi. The Katholikon is one
of the most beautiful examples of the
Greek-cross-octagon plan. This view from
the east shows the polygonal dome above
the apse. The Theotokos is typical of the
cross-in-square plan (see figure 45). The
decorative arrangement of the bricks, the
friezes, the double windows with their
arches, and the tiled lantern of the
smaller church are typical elements of the
Byzantine churches of the Greek
mainland.

71. **Interior of the Katholikon, Hosios Lukas.** *c.* 1020. Phocis, Greece. The spacious interior of the domed octagon and the cross-in-square is decorated on every available surface. The Virgin and Child are in the apses, in the dome is the scene of the Pentecost, with the apostles, partly visible, receiving the Holy Ghost from a central symbolic throne. The figures on the pendentives are the nations they evangelised.

72. **The Crucifixion.** *c.* 1020. Mosaic. Katholikon, Hosios Lukas in Phocis, Greece. The mosaics in the narthex of the church are by a different hand from those in the main body of the church. The stylisation of the figures and the way in which they stand isolated from each other by glittering gold areas seem related to the style of court workshops. The *Resurrection* (represented by the *Descent into Limbo*), the *Washing of the Feet* and *Thomas's Disbelief* are other scenes in the narthex, and in the vaults are medallions and figures of martyrs and bishops.

73 (left). **Christ Pantocrator.** 1100.
Mosaic. Daphni, Greece. This
representation usually occupies the central
dome or the main apse of Byzantine
churches. The awesome figure of Christ
Almighty is a more Eastern concept
than the suffering mortal of late Western
churches. The second person of the Holy
Trinity mediates between God and
mankind, whom he has saved and will
judge in the end.

74, 76. **Wall-paintings in Sta Sophia,
Trebizond.** *c.* 1260. Paint on plaster.
Eastern end of the Black Sea, Turkey.
During the period when the workshops at
Constantinople were comparatively
inactive after the capture of the city by the
Crusaders the far-flung outposts of the
Empire were carrying on the artistic
traditions. These fine paintings at Sta
Sophia show distinct similarities with
paintings in Macedonia and Serbia
(plates 84, 85). The common derivation
from court models can be seen in both the
attitudes and the execution of these and
the Christ Pantocrator above. *Christ among
the doctors* (below left) shows the beardless
young Christ in the same position as in
plate 12. To the left are Joseph and Mary,
and to the right the architectural detail so
typical of late Byzantine frescoes and
mosaics, especially those in Kahrie Cami.
The dramatic scene of the *Casting out of the
Devil from the daughter of the woman of
Canaan* (opposite below) shows how local
colour can increase the expression of less
familiar scenes.

75 (opposite above). **Interior of the
rock-cut church of Elmale Kilisse.**
10th century. Paint on plaster. Goreme
valley, Cappadocia, Turkey. The amazing
interiors of the chapels and churches of
the Goreme valley are carved out of the
rock with the typical architectural
elements of Byzantine churches. Here in
one of the most famous churches, the apse
is decorated with *Christ the Lawgiver*. The
angel in the dome above is separated and
surrounded by bands of decoration and
figures of saints and martyrs, prophets and
intercessors occupy the arches and
columns.

77. **Christ's entry into Jerusalem.**
12th century. Mosaic. S. Marco, Venice.
The theme is of course borrowed from
a previous model. But while the apostles
to the left are represented in an animated
fashion, the welcoming groups to the
right are more stiff. The mosaics seem to
be descended from different traditions in
a style less affected by Hellenistic trends.

78, 79 (opposite). **Noah leaves the ark.**
13th century. Mosaic. S. Marco, Venice.
The heritage of Byzantine traditions died
hard in Venice—these mosaics of the
Genesis in the cupolas of the narthex show
how a more 'conversational' religious art
developed here from the miniatures of a
6th-century Bible. Noah (above), his wife,
his sons and daughters-in-law have left
the ark beneath the protection of the
rainbow, a sign of their alliance with
God, they have released the animals
from their long captivity. Below the
scene representing **Pharaoh's dream**
shows how the architectural elements of
the later mosaics and of the Hellenistic
frescoes have influenced the Venetian
craftsmen. Pharaoh reclines while the
seven fat and seven shrivelled ears of corn
appear before him. His bed is in a
classical setting with the perspective
reversed.

80. **Apse mosaic, Torcello cathedral.**
12th century. Torcello, Venice. The
theme of the Virgin standing in a golden
apse, known from earlier examples in
churches at Nicaea and Salonika (now
destroyed), is used here with magnificent
effect. The tall elegant figure of the
Virgin dominates the apse and stands out
majestically from the gold around her.
The apostles below probably date from
earlier in the 12th century. The direct
influence of Ravenna and of Constantinople is noticeable here, as in some of
the mosaics in S. Marco, Venice. The
motif of the Virgin standing in the apse
recurs in the nearby church of Murano.

IhS · FILIAM · IAYRI · PRINCIPIS · SYNAGO
GE · I DOMO · RES VSCITAT ·

81 (opposite). **Christ healing Jairus's daughter.** 1180–90. Mosaic. Cathedral of Monreale, Palermo. The vast cycle of mosaics which cover the whole of the interior of the cathedral at Monreale were executed under the patronage of William II. The iconography and execution of the scenes points to Byzantine mosaicists, although the work may have been done by Sicilian craftsmen trained in Byzantine workshops. The elongated figures, architectural background and the grouping of Christ and the apostles to the left and the participants of the miracle to the right recall frescoes and mosaics in Constantinople. The less vivid colours and rather cramped compositions detract from their aesthetic appeal.

82, 83. **Decorative mosaics in the Palazzo Reale.** *c.* 1160–70. Palermo, Sicily. In complete contrast to the religious scenes of the Byzantine mosaics in Sicilian churches the decoration of the Norman *stanze* in the palace at Palermo shows the presence of Muslim influences in this island which had only just been liberated from the Arabs. The stylised animals, trees and hunting scenes are typical of motifs in Persian textiles. They had for a long time infiltrated into Byzantine art and the Sicilian mosaicists could easily mix the traditions.

84 (above). **Interior of the monastery church at Ravanica.** 14th century. Paint on plaster. Serbia. The effect of the frescoed churches of Macedonia and Serbia can be judged from this view of the colourful interior of the little monastery church at Ravanica. In the background is the *Crucifixion*, then in a medallion *God the Father* with the dove of the Holy Spirit. Elsewhere are rows of saints. There are signs of different hands, and some of the restoration is not faithful to the original.

85 (right). **The Deposition.** *c.* 1164. Paint on plaster. Nerezi, Macedonia. The magnificent and expressive wall-paintings at Nerezi are of exceptional quality, and were probably executed by artists from the capital. The scenes such as this *Deposition* show a desire to express plainly the emotions of the subjects and a grace and freedom of movement not hitherto found in Byzantine monumental art, but which were to have a profound effect throughout the empire.

86, 87, 88. **Three heads of Christ.** 1259.
Paint on plaster. Church of St Nicholas,
Boiana, near Sofia, Bulgaria. These three
representations of Christ show the
personal approach of the paintings: the
infant Christ (left), shown without his
mother, is an enchantingly human child,
such as is seldom found in Byzantine
painting. The youthful head from the
scene of *Christ among the Doctors* is a
powerfully expressive image, while that
of *Christ Blessing* is more traditional in
approach but equally personal in feeling.

89. **Sevastocrator Kaloian and
Sevastocratoress Desislava.** 1259.
Paint on plaster. Church of St Nicholas,
Boiana, near Sofia, Bulgaria. The
influence of Constantinople is still
evident in the wall-paintings which cover
this attractive Bulgarian church. There is
however a new preoccupation with
emotions, with realism and naturalistic
detail; these are obviously portraits. Here
the Sevastocrator presents a model of the
church of St Nicholas, who is depicted
on his left. The Sevastocratoress lifts
her hands in prayer. Both the figures
wear the richly embroidered garments of
the 13th-century Bulgarian boyars.

90. **Christ Emmanuel.** *c.* 1300–20. Mosaic. Kahrie Cami (Chora Church), Constantinople. This church was rebuilt in the 11th century as it now stands and decorated during the two hundred years which followed. Most of the mosaic decoration was executed at the same time, among which the two panels above the doors of the narthex representing Christ and the Virgin. Although the attitude of Christ is traditional, his features are less severe, no longer the dreaded Pantocrator, but the refuge of mankind.

91 (below). **Detail of the Birth of the Virgin.** *c.* 1300–20. Mosaic. Kahrie Cami (Chora Church), Constantinople. The story of the Virgin is one of the main themes of the mosaic decoration preserved at Kahrie Cami. The wealth of architectural details, the furniture and the activity of the figures gives a dramatic effect to the scenes. This detail is particularly realistic with the cradle prepared to the left, the anxious father peeping to the right and the preparation for the washing of the Virgin to the extreme right.

92. **Joachim, Anna and Mary.** *c.* 1300
or 1320. Mosaic. Kahrie Cami (Chora
Church), Constantinople. The vault
mosaics show the same preoccupation
with architectural details. For the first
time in Christian art these mosaics show
a scene of familial tenderness—the
parents of the Virgin caress the little
child who is to be the Theotokos—the
mother of God.

93 (below). **The Anastasis.** *c.* 1305.
Paint on plaster. Kahrie Cami (Chora
Church), Constantinople. The *parecclesion*,
or small chapel, which runs the length of
the Chora church is decorated with
magnificent frescoes concerned with
death or the after-life. This *Resurrection*, or
Descent of Christ into Limbo, is in the apse.
The larger crowd of people, the width of
movement and the vivid colours lend
drama to the traditional iconography.

These diverse tendencies were to continue without a break through into Romanesque art, which with its power of expression brought them together and transformed them into a vigorous new style.

MINIATURES AND MANUSCRIPTS

Even if the western mosaicists and mural painters did possess a certain originality, they never had the disconcerting power of their contemporary miniaturists. It is rare to find such violent contrasts between two arts of the same period. The reason is that from the 8th century the miniature had undergone the influence of Ireland which had not touched monumental art.

The so-called 'Echternach' Gospel-book, which was painted about 690 in Ireland or in an Irish abbey in England, was brought by the monks to the abbey founded by Willibrord in 698 at Echternach. More even than the Durrow Book, it subordinates the human figure to an interplay of curls and volutes. Many other original documents, just as characteristic, arrived in the Frankish kingdom in this way.

There are few works as intellectually stimulating as these miniatures, in which this 'insular' art confronts Mediterranean art on its own ground. This convergence is already apparent in works of English origin, like the *Codex Aureus* of Stockholm, painted at Canterbury about 750, in which there are portraits of the Evangelists, sitting quietly beneath arcatures decorated with motifs taken from ornamental mosaics like the wavy ribbons and in others where the 'insular' decoration is applied to a heavily framed text. Also in works like the Gospel-book of Trier (Trèves) cathedral, painted at Echternach about 730, the 'insular' decoration is more disciplined and arranged so as to leave room for animals—the symbols of the four Evangelists—enclosed in frames. In the way they are

94, 95, 96 (opposite). **Mistra.** c. 1350. Peloponnese, Greece. The ruins of the little town of Mistra are scattered over the foothills of the Taygetus and look out over the plain of Sparta. The town was ceded by the Franks to Michael Palaeologus at the end of the 13th century and most of the wall-paintings date from the 14th century. **The church of the Pantanassa** (below left) follows the plan of Byzantine churches and with its textured exterior, its main and secondary domes and the paintings of the interior is typical of the churches scattered throughout the town. **The Raising of Lazarus** (above) is from the Pantanassa church. Here the depth and dramatic effect of these 14th-century frescoes can be seen to full advantage. The figure of Christ to the left and the resurrected Lazarus (to the right) still in his shroud are set against a rocky landscape. **The vaults of the Peribleptos** (below right) are covered with magnificent paintings: *Christ Pantocrator* in the blue dome, and on the surrounding arches the *Ascension*, the *Nativity*, the *Baptism*, the *Transfiguration*, the *Last Supper*, *Thomas's doubting* and the *Pentecost*. All the scenes are executed with a wealth of detail, great freedom of movement, and in brilliant colours.

drawn, these animals remind one of their predecessors, which were incorporated into the design. It is not surprising therefore to find basic motifs of Irish origin on metal or ivory reliquaries made in the Frankish empire.

When Charlemagne decided to create an official workshop at court for the reproduction of manuscripts, his painters were also to find themselves confronted by these different tendencies—and each of them was affected in his own way. It was the Gospel-book of Godescalc, commanded by Charlemagne returning from Rome in 781, after the baptism of his son Pepin, that marked the opening of the royal workshop. Like the great imperial manuscripts of Constantinople, it is written in gold and silver on purple parchment. It contains Christ in Majesty and the four Evangelists. The composition is traditional, but the execution is Italian-influenced, using a great range of colours, which contrasts vividly with both previous western illustration and Byzantine miniature painting.

A whole series of masterpieces was to emerge from the palace chapel, among which are admirable portraits of the Evangelists, sitting diagonally on a seat that seems to be part of the architecture, and which have an intense vitality of their own; they are shown in magnificent arcades, with their symbolic animals (the Gospel-book of St Médard de Soissons). There are also portraits of enthroned emperors, surrounded by officials and ecclesiastics, which are reminiscent of classical art. Some years later, a new palace school was to rediscover even older techniques as in the so-called Coronation Gospels which was almost a return to classical painting; there are several manuscripts that revived this technique.

Curiously enough, these highly graphic works seem to have brought about a revival in draughtsmanship. The Ebbo Gospel-book, at Reims, marks the flowering of a new sensibility—a desire on the part of the artists not to stylise, as they drew them, the folds that they had just learnt to paint. This resulted in the Utrecht Psalter, drawn at Reims about 820, which represents a complete revolution in artistic habits. The psalms are illustrated not according to their general meaning, nor according to the historical events of their composition, but by seizing upon every allusion as it occurs in each verse. As a result, the pages are covered by a mass of strangely realistic figures depicted against a background of mountains or dream architecture, side by side with cleverly dramatised allegorical interpretations. Some scholars believe that the miniaturist had recourse to early Christian models, and one is constantly reminded of earlier works, but everything has been assimilated. It is the astonishing draughtsmanship which gives unity to the illustrations of the volume and they are executed in such an original way that one is tempted to abandon any attempt at trying to discover its origin. (see The Medieval World, figure 22)

Each of these series of paintings turned back to ancient sources, but all of them go beyond those sources: we are no longer in early Christian art but in the Middle Ages.

The Byzantine Expansion

In the East a magnificent revival of Byzantine power in the 9th century almost coincided with the end of the iconoclastic dispute. Michael III and his uncle, Bardas, intensified the policy of converting the Slavs, to whom Cyril and Methodius brought not only the Gospel but also an alphabet created specially for them. He then helped his new favourite, Basil, to eliminate Bardas; Basil in his turn became so powerful that he was able to rid himself of his protector and found the Macedonian dynasty. This dynasty was to enjoy a brilliant reign from the end of the 9th century to the middle of the 11th. In 880, Byzantium regained the positions it had lost in Italy. Basil II rid the Balkans of the threats from Bulgarians and Russians. Nicephorus II drove out the Arabs, reconquering first Cilicia, then Syria, Armenia and Cyprus were reoccupied. A powerful empire was thus reconstituted and its glory was to increase, and its art spread accordingly. Even in regions like Sicily, where the Normans had established a kingdom that was strong enough to hold both Arabs and Byzantines in awe, basilical churches of an almost western type were decorated with Byzantine mosaics by Greek artists.

The starting point of this new expansion was obviously Constantinople and above all H. Sophia, which was given a new imperial decoration. Mosaics covered the walls of the narthex and gallery, celebrating the accession of emperors and empresses like the imperial statues in the forums of earlier times: once again the icon replaced the idol and painting—or in this case mosaic—replaced sculpture in the round. At the west gate, Leo VI (886–912) is represented prostrated before Christ in majesty, seated on a golden throne, between medallions in which the Virgin and an angel enact the scene of the Annunciation. At the south gate where the Virgin is shown between Constantine and Justinian, the two former emperors look like brothers, dressed alike in purple tunics and long, cleverly draped, golden stoles. Leo VI is given a beard and represents a transition from the imaginary portrait to the real one.

In 1030, the Emperor Romanos III and the Empress Zoe were represented, in the south gallery, on either side of Christ. After the death of her second husband, Zoe married Constantine Monomachus, who, in turn, became emperor; as with the statues of the Roman emperors, whose marble heads were removable, all that was necessary was for the face of the emperor to be changed.

The Comneni followed the example of the Macedonians: as did John II Comnenus and the Empress Irene in 1118. Adding to these the splendid frontispieces of books painted in the court studios, we have a rich series of imperial portraits, including those of Basil II in the Venice psalter and of Nicephorus Botaniates (1078) in the Homilies of St John Chrysostom. All these pictures are static and utterly imperial; and the art of the court overshadows the religious art.

Basil II had a new church built at Constantinople—the Nea—which was later destroyed. It is thought to have

78. **The Emperor Constantine II and the Empress Zoe.** 1030. Mosaic. South gallery, H. Sophia, Constantinople. The mosaic originally portrayed Romanos III who was already Zoe's second husband. It was enough just to change the head to portray her third. The sovereigns present Christ with a bag of gold and a donation—for God's protection of the imperial family.

provided the model for another church, the Assumption at Nicaea, which was destroyed in 1922, but of which photographs have been preserved. These show a group of archangels and a particularly fine picture of the Virgin, standing on a plinth and holding the Christ Child in front of her, in a vast golden dome. This simple composition was used later at Murano and at Torcello—and produces an astonishing effect of grandeur.

BYZANTINE MOSAICS IN GREECE

Three Greek churches also provide evidence of the splendour of the 'Macedonian Renaissance'. All three are monastery churches: Hosios Lukas in Phocis (early 11th century), the Nea Moni at Chios (about 1050) and the monastery of Daphni on the road from Athens to Eleusis. Such monastic enterprises may be regarded as being independent of the art of the court, they may have been realised by Greek artists foreign to the capital. It is all the more remarkable to find in them touches that are peculiar to the early Byzantine inspiration of this period.

The church of the monastery of St Luke—Hosios Lukas —has a central dome, dominated by a medallion of the Christ Pantocrator, surrounded by archangels and prophets. In the apse, is a seated *Virgin*. Above her, in a dome, the apostles, sitting in a circle, are receiving the illumina-

79a, b. **Daphni.** Second half of the 11th century. Greece. The golden walls of the monastery church of Daphni (b) surrounded by pines and cypress trees, stand out against the barren hillside. (a) The magnificent mosaics inside are ablaze with gold (see plate 73). The crucifixion is most expressive in its restrained treatment.

tion of the Holy Ghost. In the niches placed beneath the dome are represented the Annunciation, the Nativity, the Presentation in the Temple and the Baptism in the Jordan. In the narthex, opposite the entrance, is the Crucifixion—Christ on the cross, with the Virgin and St John, the Resurrection, represented by the descent into limbo and, at the ends of the gallery, the Washing of the Feet and Thomas's Disbelief. This series of historical scenes is complemented by a whole army of saints and bishops—intercessors and witnesses—on the vaults, on the arches and at the tops of the walls.

In the Gospel scenes, there is an added dignity. This is apparent in the attitude of Christ in Limbo: he is shown full-face, yet, despite the effort he is making to pull Adam from his grave, there is no loss of balance. His gesture is that of the conquering emperor—the spear being replaced by the cross—standing over his defeated enemy, represented here by the gaping jaws of hell. On the other hand, the Nativity is narrative and picturesque, with connecting motifs on a different scale.

The scenes in the Nea Moni—the New Monastery—on the island of Chios are perhaps closer to the models at Constantinople (1042). One is struck by the red eye-lids and green shadows on the face of the Virgin, who rests her cheek on Christ's hand as he is taken down from the cross. Moreover, this face has a clever, and sorrowful dissymmetry. The features of Christ, St John and the angel are more impassive—as in a very fine picture of the Baptism.

The monastery at Daphni, like many in the West, but *79b* like even more in the East, looks like an oasis. The dome rises over gold and white walls, between tall pines and cypresses, and the mosaics greet the visitor in a blaze of light, although they themselves are grave, somewhat cold **73** —one might almost say classical. The Crucifixion, for *79a* example, is surprisingly sober. As at Hosios Lukas, the Crucifix, the Virgin and St John are each treated in isolation. St John is presented like a statue—which suggests antecedents beyond Christian art, in ancient Greek sculpture. The attitude of the Virgin is traditional but the face, shown in semi-profile raised towards the cross, is charged with controlled suffering. The Christ on the cross is also treated with restraint—the body curves only slightly to one side, the musculature hardly visible, and his eyes are closed in an almost serene expression. This beautiful picture is full of respectful adoration.

It is rather surprising to find the same discretion—in this case perhaps as a result of a certain lack of feeling—in scenes like Thomas's disbelief, in which the risen Christ, so much taller than his apostles, offers himself impassively for verification, while the apostles stand around looking detached and distinguished. The Anastasis, which is more dramatic in plan, manages to create emotion only on the face of Eve. In the Entry into Jerusalem, the handsome face of Christ has a faraway look and there is a frozen quality about the enthusiastic gestures and noble faces of the onlookers. There is no stiffness here: the technique is faultless but the feeling is always controlled. At Daphni, Byzantine art is revealed as the expression of an accomplished civilisation.

All these monuments, whether imperial or monastic, give an impression of dignity, discretion and nobility. The influence of a courtly art can be felt even in distant monasteries. It is the same impression that one gets when turning the pages of the great imperial manuscripts of the time, the

80. **Sta Sophia,** Trebizond. Before 1260. Situated on the far-flung south-east shore of the Black Sea this is one of the few surviving examples of Byzantine architecture under the Palaeologues. The basic domed cross-in-square plan has been expanded by projecting porches to the north, west and south (seen in this view). The interior is decorated with frescoes (see plates 74, 76).

100
69 Paris psalter 139, the Venice psalter or the Homilies of Gregory Nazianzus—all works in which the religious emotion is contained within the purity of style. Classical echoes crop up constantly, not only when the personified figure of the Jordan appears in the river, or that of Night participates in the prophet's vision. It is difficult not to be affected by this charm—even if one prefers more powerful works, less dependent on Hellenistic tradition.

THE SPREAD OF BYZANTINE ART

The taking of Constantinople by the Crusaders in 1204 interrupted the development of Byzantine art in the capital for half a century. But it did not die—any more than the empire of which it was the expression. It seems that when the artists were forced to flee they simply set up their studios elsewhere.

First of all, they followed those members of the imperial family who had succeeded in escaping and establishing their authority in some more or less distant province of the decapitated empire. They went first to Nicaea, on the far shore of the Bosphorus, where Theodorus Lascaris had a patriarch elected to crown him emperor. Despite the efforts of Baldwin, the Latin emperor, he succeeded in maintaining his position, but not in regrouping under his authority all the territories that had been left unconquered by the Franks. A 'despotate' was established in Epirus, and another empire at Trebizond, with Alexis and David Comnenus, who considered themselves to be the representatives of the legitimate dynasty.

During Constantinople's period of silence, it was under them that Byzantine art was allowed to continue its devel-
74, 76 opment, as is apparent in the fine paintings of Sta Sophia at
80 Trebizond (1260), recently brought to light under the direction of Professor Talbot Rice, by the removal of the plaster that covered them. These paintings, unfortunately incomplete, reveal a perfect technical mastery and elegance of form; and among the usual traditional themes curious innovations in detail are to be found. But what is most striking about them is their close relation to the paintings that emerged in Macedonia at the same time and in which there is the same freshness of inspiration, the same

concern with expression—in short, an enrichment and understanding of the subjects.

CAPPADOCIA

Although the contribution of Cappadocia to the history of Christian painting is so great, its position does not seem to have been properly appreciated. This is not because the works are undated, but rather because their conception and execution are so original that they continue to be regarded as 'a new province of Byzantine art', as the Rev. Father Jerphanion writes in the title of the book in which he published them.

These frescoes decorate 'rupestrian' churches—that is, churches carved out of rock. They were not natural caves, which, as in Egypt or Syria, were inhabited by anchorites; the strange countryside of the Urgub region, west of Caesarea, for example, is dotted with rocky cones, and generally dwellings were carved out of vertical rock faces. *81a* The same method was adopted for the innumerable churches of the region—and these artificial caves used the traditional church forms. There are chapels with a single nave, true basilicas, and cruciform churches, with one or several domes. The whole structure is always cut out of the rock. On the outside, the façades are very restrained in style—generally a simple entrance surmounted by a horse-shoe arch. Even the monasteries may be entirely subterranean, the refectories, the monks' cells and the workshops, as well as the chapels. It is, in fact, a false architecture, *81b, c* enriched by the continuous cycles of paintings that cover its walls.
75

From the first half of the 7th century, the Byzantine province of Cappadocia was threatened by the Arabs, who held the upper Euphrates and the Taurus passes and sent raids into Asia Minor. The country enjoyed one period of peace, from the reign of Michael III and particularly that of Basil I (867) to the approach of the Seljuks (1060). It was only from 1210, when the power of the Seljuks had been weakened, that peace returned to the country, and lasted until at least the end of the century.

Some groups of buildings are decorated only with abstract motifs: geometrical shapes or foliated scrolls.

133

81a, b. The rock-cut churches of Cappadocia.
Turkey. *(a)* The Goreme valley is composed of extraordinary
rock formations in which dwellings and churches have been
carved. *(b)* The rock is hollowed out to form the domes and
apses, naves and aisles of normal church plans. The elaborate
arcades of Toqale Kilisse are an example of this. The
11th-century paintings reveal a lower layer of non-figurative
decoration probably done during the Iconoclasm. *(c)* The
Crucifixion is a typical subject for the lunettes of these churches.

82. **The interior of S. Marco,** Venice. 12th century. The glorious glittering effect of the interior of the great Venetian basilica is achieved by the almost total decoration of the walls with mosaics (see plates 77, 78, 79). The tall lanterns of the dome are pierced with windows. The basilica was modelled on the church of the Holy Apostles, built by Justinian in Constantinople.

83 (opposite). **S. Marco,** Venice. 10th–11th centuries. The aerial view shows the five domes of the basilica forming a Greek cross. The height of the lead covering and the shape of the lanterns give the building its entirely original character.

These have been attributed to the iconoclastic period. Using the iconography as an indicator, scholars have claimed that some of the buildings date from before the crisis. Nevertheless, it is from the Macedonian period that churches, themselves perhaps of an earlier date, were decorated with the figurative paintings that made them famous. There are enough inscriptions to enable us to distinguish the dates of several series of works and to classify them accordingly—from the 10th to the 13th century and even later. The earliest dedication, at Tavchanle Kilisse, mentions Constantine Porphyrogenetes and seems to date from the years 913–20. Around this example a whole series of buildings had been grouped, particularly among the churches of the Goreme valley (Qalecar Kilisse, Toqale Kilisse, etc.). Another group, from the 11th century, comprises the columned churches of Goreme, and shows a growing Byzantine influence. With the Seljuk invasion in the 12th century, the paintings diminish in number and in quality: in the interpretation of the models, which had previously come from Byzantium, there was a return to popular tradition. In the 13th century there was a new period of great activity: several very richly decorated churches date from between 1222 (Souvasa) and 1293 (Ortakeuy).

In examining closely these Cappadocian paintings, one is struck less perhaps by these differences than by the characteristics they share in common. The themes and models adopted in Constantinople are recognisable, and this or that detail from Qaraback Kilisse, for example, is particularly close to them. But, in the boldness, the hasty execution and the brilliance of the colour, one generally feels that one is being confronted by an interpretation that is not only local, but popular in tradition. The models are there, but the artists use them in their own way, within the bounds of a common style: the figures are very tall and occupy the whole pictorial area. Again, architecture fills the few gaps there are. There is no question of artistic refinements, of delicate effects of light and shade or of originality in expression. They are bold, simple pictures, some-

times, in the later period, as at Balleq Kilisse, almost childish, each one treats its subject both powerfully and with restraint and never forgets the role that the picture must play in the motley of the building.

In the domes, one finds the Pantocrator, or the Christ of the Ascension, being carried in his mandorla by angels, and, below, the circle of apostles, with upturned heads. In the niches are the Virgin and Child, either standing or sitting. In the lunettes one might see a Nativity or a Crucifixion, then, on superimposed borders, complete cycles, such as the life of the Virgin, the Childhood of Christ, Christ's miracles or the Passion. There are also lives of the saints—of St Simeon Stylites at Zilve or St Barbara at Soghanle, the patrons of their respective churches—or rows of portraits of apostles, prophets or bishops. These may also be found in the keystone of a vault, as busts in medallions.

81c

Within each group of churches the iconography does not seem to vary a great deal perhaps because they were decorated by the same painter or the same studio or perhaps because of local imitation. Details like the form of the water of the Jordan in the scene of the Baptism or the arrangement of the apostles in the Ascension makes these connections more obvious. Certain scenes are treated with a particular fullness, like the Blessing of the Apostles, shown in two rows facing the spectator, or upright along the sides of a vault, with Christ advancing in the middle. The forty Martyrs of Sebaste, in the church that bears their name, are arranged in the same way.

But it is the total impression that is most striking: this decoration covering everything, sometimes cleverly split up according to the architectural components—arches, tympana, vaults and domes—accentuated by borders, or sometimes, on the contrary, without any break between the scenes. Even more than at Monreale or at Kahrie Cami, the iconography overwhelms the worshipper with its crowd of saints and its accumulation of pictures.

ITALY

Under the Macedonians, Italy knew two episodes in her

relations with the Byzantine Empire that were to be of great importance in her history.

The Byzantines witnessed first the formation, then the expansion of the power of Venice. The empire still held Dalmatia and its presence was a break on Venetian expansion. But the Carolingians and their successors represented a much more immediate danger: so much so that the Doges usually preferred an alliance with Byzantium, which opened up trading routes to the East. In every episode in the struggles of the Macedonians and the Comneni against the Bulgarians, the Arabs and the Normans, Venice played a role that was often a determining one. But whether protected, in alliance, or hostile, Venice was nonetheless affected by her relations with the metropolis on the Bosphorus.

This explains how there began, around 1100, the building of the cathedral of S. Marco and the first stages of its mosaic decoration.

83   S. Marco in Venice is a church with five domes arranged in the form of a cross. It is encircled by a side-aisle, with columns between the pillars. At the east end this side-aisle is transformed into side chapels, so the church thus has three apses. An exterior portico, covered by a series of small domes, surrounds the west arm to create five doorways very deep in the façade, covered with small columns: in the ground-plan they form the *scenae frons* of a Roman theatre —alternate square and semi-circular niches. This structure, of which the general arrangement is taken from the church of the Holy Apostles at Constantinople, as rebuilt by Justinian, creates a fine effect in itself. This is enhanced on the outside by the later superelevation of the lead domes and on the inside—as in the narthex, by the brilliance of

82   the mosaics.

Of course the mosaics were laid at different times, and added to, repaired and re-arranged. Here and there one might find a baroque saint, with billowing clothes, but the gold backgrounds were left untouched and the effect remains. The domes, 'shining with their own, unearthly

light' (Marcel Proust) are best seen from the interior galleries. Questions of iconography and chronology are then forgotten; Byzantine architecture is balance, but it is also colour.

There is little doubt that Byzantine tradition, represented for the *Genesis* in the narthex for example by the 6th-century Cotton Bible, was, from the 12th century, interpreted by the Venetians in their own way; however they wished to remain faithful to it. But it seems it would be better to say that there is a Venetian School of Byzantine mosaic.

The scenes which are definitely old inside the church were distributed between different studios. In the Temptation of Christ or the Entry into Jerusalem, the style is full of 77 simplicity and nobility; whereas in the Ascension of the central dome, it revives with vigour and movement the theme illustrated at St Sophia of Salonika—the apostles run about gesticulating as they watch their Master rise into the sky and, below them, between the windows, the Virtues and Beatitudes remind one of dancers, while the calm evangelists, in the pendentives, are by another hand.

The 13th-century Genesis in the domes of the narthex is still a delightful series despite its having been considerably retouched. The Creation, the Fall and the Flood have 78, 79 an apparently naive, but effective expression, owing to the precision of the drawing and the technique of the placing of the cubes: the animals in the ark, the rain falling on the drowned and the spires sticking up out of the water as Noah releases the dove are quite unforgettable.

The Venetian School was also active at Torcello, on an 80 island in the lagoon, where two masterpieces face each other: the golden apse dating from the 12th century, in which stands a slender, blue Virgin presenting the Child, above a row of apostles, faces the inside wall of the façade, which is taken up by an extraordinary Last Judgement, with five registers of increasing height, dominated by the traditional scene of the Resurrection—Christ's descent into Limbo, flanked by two angels dressed as imperial dignitaries. Above, Christ is enthroned among his apostles;

below, angels separate the saved from the damned—an arrangement of scenes already treated, but linked together for the first time in an impressive whole.

SICILY

The second event of great importance to Italy was the conquest of Sicily, first by the Arabs, then by the Normans. It was in 827, while the Muslims of Egypt were occupying Crete, that the Muslims of Africa made a victorious attack on Sicily. In spite of successive counter-attacks the Byzantine positions were gradually eroded. The Normans, who were first brought into this struggle as mercenaries, soon established their power both in Apulia and Sicily. The Comneni were forced to negotiate with them in 1073, and in 1172, to offer them Porphyrogenetes in marriage. Roger II, king of the two Sicilies from 1130 to 1154, negotiated on an equal level with both the Byzantine empire and the empire of the West.

The contacts that had been created by such a succession of crises had given birth in Sicily to a very complex art. Its architecture is sometimes of a western type as in the basilicas at Cefalù and Monreale. On the other hand, the Martorana at Palermo, a delightful domed church, is very Byzantine inside but takes on Islamic forms on the outside.

A great many of the mosaics around Palermo have been preserved. This is partly due to the Byzantine artists who were followed by Sicilian mosaicists on the spot. As a result there are disparities and inequalities of style, which are apparent on close examination, but which detract very little from the overall effect. The cathedral at Cefalù is the

84. **Christ crowning Roger II.** 1143–1151. Mosaic. Church of the Martorana, Palermo. Roger II was the Norman king of Sicily. The scene of investiture was borrowed from the official court art of Constantinople (see figure 78) while the picture itself may have been executed by a Greek mosaicist.

oldest of these buildings—it was begun in 1131. In the apse, a calm-faced Christ Pantocrator holds out a Bible to the faithful, on which the text 'I am the light of the world' is written, on one side in Latin and on the other in Greek. But there is nothing Latin about his features or his attitude. Below him is the Virgin enthroned among the archangels, then the bishops and saints—a traditional arrangement. In the cathedral at Monreale, built about 1190, we find the Pantocrator in the apse, then the Virgin, surrounded by angels and saints. But the nave, the transept above the arches, between the windows of the clerestory, the walls of the side aisles and, finally, the façade wall are covered with historical mosaic pictures recounting in detail the Old and New Testaments. The iconography is traditional; **81** the execution is robust and retains a character of narrative imagery, with no striving after expression. The backgrounds of architecture and landscape, the attitudes of the figures and the costumes all seem to conform to the norms. The colour is bright, and occasionally a more interesting figure or a livelier scene appears.

The mosaics of the Martorana at Palermo are of a finer quality, and their position in the structure of a Byzantine church allows them more variety and charm. The Palatine Chapel, the jewel of Roger II's palace, is decorated beneath Moorish ceilings and a dome supported by squinches, with evangelists, rows of saints with faces resembling the originals of Constantinople and scenes along the walls. They have a freshness which is more appealing than those at Monreale. The Byzantine Christ is shown crowning Roger II in the narthex of the Martorana, and **84** William II at Monreale. The Norman kings are wearing the same costume as the emperors in the coronation scenes in Constantinople. They showed their greatness by borrowing not only the emperors' clothes, but also their artists.

They also borrowed extensively from the Arabs: in a hall of the palace at Palermo one is surprised to encounter whole series of hunting and animal scenes, set among trees, **82,83** which recall certain pavement compositions in Antioch, borrowed from the Sassanians under Justinian, but in their Islamic version. The taste of the Norman princes for rich fabrics which resulted in the establishing of weaving-shops, was no doubt also responsible for their importing silks not only from Byzantium, but also from Persia.

This eclecticism of the Norman princes, which is like a reflection of the history of Sicily from the 9th to the 12th century, produces a delightfully exotic effect. The traveller may not feel, as he does in Venice, that he is in an entirely different world, but he cannot fail to be aware here of the confrontation of cultures.

THE SLAVS

The People's Commissar for the Red Army who, on 2 May 1944, liberated the camp of Malchow in Mecklenburg, in the heart of Germany, where a few survivors from the terrible camp at Dora had ended up, said to the professor of Byzantine civilisation who received him in the name of his fellow-prisoners: 'I hope that you will soon resume

(Continued on page 153)

97 (above). **Eliezer and Rebecca.**
6th century. Purple parchment.
National Library, Vienna. Known as the
Vienna Genesis this famous manuscript is
one of the rare examples of early
Byzantine illumination and is of uncertain
date and provenance. But even if there is
nothing definite with which to compare it
the taste for anecdote and landscape is
Alexandrian. Rebecca leaves the town,
approaching the spring, and gives water
to Jacob's messenger before watering her
camels. The text is illustrated with an
uninterrupted movement, in a charming
and informal way.

98 (left). **Christ before Pilate.** 6th
century. Purple parchment. 12 × 10½ in.
(30·7 × 26 cm.). Cathedral Treasure,
Rossano, Italy. The Rossano Codex has
the same continuity of imagery as in the
Vienna Genesis. In this instance the scenes
appear more detached from each other.
Pilate in the upper register hears the case
of the chief priests. Below, to the left,
Judas is overcome with remorse and
hands back the thirty silver pieces; on the
right he has hanged himself. The solemn
symmetry of the judgement scene is
followed by others in a more intimate
style.

ᾗ οἴα μὴ τῆς μακαρίας διαγωγῆς
τὴν ταλαιπωρίαν ἀμή·

99 (opposite). **Sermons of the Monk James Kokkinobaphos.** 12th century. 9 × 6 in. (23 × 16·5 cm.). Bibliothèque Nationale, Paris (MS. Grec. 1208 fo. 47). The expulsion of Adam and Eve from Paradise is here depicted in a delightfully original way. The *Sermons on the Virgin* by James Kokkinobaphos is a series of discussions taken from the Gospels and the Apocrypha. All the illustrations are treated in the same spontaneous and masterly way. Their importance lies in the complete originality of the iconography.

100 (above). **The Penitence of David.** 10th century. Manuscript. 14⅛ × 10¼ in. (36 × 26 cm.). Bibliothèque Nationale, Paris (MS. Grec. 139). The miniatures of the famous Paris Psalter which came from the imperial workshops at Constantinople were evidently copied from an earlier manuscript and as with many manuscripts of the same period seemed a direct continuation of classical art. In this scene David, reproached by the prophet Nathan, repents at having abducted Bathsheba. On the right is a personification of penitence, an Alexandrian tradition.

✝ H ΔΓΔ ΚΥ̅ ΜΚ̅ Ζ̅ ΠΔG ✝

ΕΚ Τ̅Υ̅ ΚΑΤΆ Ι(Ω):

Ν αρχη̅ η̅μο/ ό υ̅
Καὶ ὁ λόγος η̅ μ π̅
τὸν θ̅ν̅ καὶ θ̅c̅ η̅ν̅

ὁ λόγος ✝ ο υ̅τος η̅ν̅
ὸ ν αρχ ι̅ π̅ρὸς τὸν
θ̅ν̅ ✝ π αν τ α δι αυ̅
τοῦ ἐ γ ἐ+ καὶ χ
ρὶς αὐτοῦ ἐγεν̅ετο

101 (opposite). **The Lectionary of the Gospels.** 11th century. Manuscript. 13½ × 10 in. (33 × 25 cm.). Pierpont Morgan Library, New York. This typical chapter-heading begins the Gospel of St John. Left, the *Descent into Limbo*, the *Anastasis*, and on the right the inspired Evangelist dictates his book. The scenes are enclosed in an elaborate decorative frame and head the two columns of text, which was to remain an accepted arrangement in later manuscripts.

102 (above). **The Throne of Maximian.** *c.* 550. Ivory. 59 × 24 in. (150 × 60·5 cm.). The Archiepiscopal Museum, Ravenna. Maximian was Archbishop of Ravenna from 545 to 553 which dates the throne itself. It is however made up of a number of plaques of different styles which have given rise to some discussion as to their provenance. The intricately carved foliated scroll either side of the monogram, peopled with birds and animals, has a distinctly

classical flavour. The panels on the front of the throne depicting St John the Baptist and the Evangelists are by two different hands and the narrative plaques have a varied and original iconography especially in the scenes from the life of Joseph which was a popular Egyptian theme.

103. **The Holy Women at the Sepulchre.** 5th century. Ivory. $12\frac{1}{8} \times 5\frac{1}{4}$ in. (31×13.5 cm.). Trivulzio Collection, Castello Sforzesco, Milan. The simple beauty of this early carving on the leaf of a diptych is characteristic of the passage from classical to Christian art. The two scenes, one above the other, represent two moments in the action, the sleeping guards, then the angel greeting the Holy Women at the entrance to the tomb. The risen Christ is not featured— Christian art proceeds by allusions. The tomb recalls the *aediculum* built over the Holy Sepulchre in the 4th century. Note the Christian scenes on the doors.

104 (opposite). **The Harbaville Triptych** (detail). 10th century. Ivory. *c.* $9\frac{1}{2} \times 5\frac{1}{2}$ in. (24×14 cm.). Louvre, Paris. The central panel of this outstanding example of Byzantine ivory carving shows Christ enthroned between the Virgin and John the Baptist in the upper register. In the lower register and on the other panels are apostles and saints with prophets in medallions. In spite of the simplicity of the composition and the traditional attitude of the characters the delicate execution gives an astonishing variety of detail. The technical perfection of ivory carvings was maintained through the ages.

105 (left). **The Beresford Hope Cross.** 9th century. Cloisonné enamel on gold, mounted in silver gilt. $3\frac{3}{8} \times 2\frac{1}{4}$ in. (8×5 cm.). Victoria and Albert Museum, London. This small Italo-Byzantine reliquary of the True Cross shows the technique of cloisonné enamel to full effect. These colourful inlays were a favourite form of decoration in Byzantine reliquaries and precious objects. The Virgin with her arms outstretched is between St Peter and St Andrew, St John the Baptist above, and St Paul. The other side shows Christ on the Cross between the Virgin and St John.

106 (below). **The Stavelot Triptych.** *c.* 1150. Copper, silver gilt, champlevé enamels. $12\frac{1}{2} \times 25$ in. (31×63 cm.). Pierpont Morgan Library, New York. This portable altarpiece was made by Godefroid de Claire for the Abbot of Stavelot. The small Byzantine enamel triptychs set into the centre were probably made at Constantinople for relics of the True Cross. The upper small triptych is $2\frac{3}{8} \times 4\frac{1}{2}$ in. (6×11 cm.) and the lower $4\frac{1}{2} \times 7\frac{7}{8}$ in. (11×20 cm.). The enamels in the two leaves are later, and probably of Western workmanship.

Portable reliquaries in ivory or in gold and silver played an important part in the spread of Byzantine art together with manuscripts and icons.

107 (opposite). **Pala d'Oro.** 10th–14th centuries. Enamels mounted in gold and silver Gothic framework, set with precious stones. Basilica of S. Marco, Venice. This detail from the glorious altarpiece of S. Marco shows the centre of the elaborate panel, and the magnificent late Byzantine plaque of Christ, enthroned in the familiar attitude of the Lawgiver.

The roundels surrounding it contain the four Evangelists; above are scenes of the *Baptism*, the *Last Supper*, the *Crucifixion* and the *Resurrection*, and the symbol of the Holy Ghost. Saints and martyrs occupy the surrounding niches. The enamels were brought from Constantinople in the 10th century and again at the beginning of the 13th after the capture of the city. The present setting dates from 1345 and includes much earlier elements in its Gothic frame. It conforms to the taste for magnificence that the Venetians acquired from the Byzantines.

110 (above). **Woven Byzantine silk.** 10th century. Silk compound twill. 12½ × 11¼ in. (31 × 28 cm.). Victoria and Albert Museum, London. The extreme fragility of woven silks and textiles has left only rare examples to posterity, which of course arouse the interest and controversy of scholars. Imperial silks were dyed in purple, but fragments of other magnificent fabrics purportedly from Byzantine workshops do exist (see figure 95). They were usually found in tombs shrouding emperors, saints or bishops. This beautiful fragment shows the Persian elements so common in Byzantine textiles, the confronted dog-birds isolated in roundels.

111 (above). **Christ and St Menas.**
6th century. Paint on panel. Louvre,
Paris. The striking icon from the
Monastery of St Catherine, Mount Sinai
(see plate 46) is an example of the more
provincial style of Coptic art, to be
compared with that of the textiles in
plates 108, 109. The same love of bright
colours, especially in the green (now
faded) and the brilliant yellows, and red.
The informality of the figures contrasts
with the frontality, the lack of proportion,
and the sense of divinity conveyed by the
symmetrical faces with their huge, staring
eyes.

112 (opposite). **The Virgin of Vladimir.**
c. 1125. Paint on panel. The Tretyakov
Gallery, Moscow. The compassionate
quality of the icon known as *Our Lady of
Vladimir* was unknown to the painter of
the icon above, and to the earlier
Byzantine icon painters, for whom the
Virgin and Child were symbols of the
faith. This human and tender attitude
and the exquisite execution of the
painting were to have a far-reaching
influence; for the *Virgin of Vladimir*,
although painted in Constantinople,
was later taken to Russia and set a trend
for Russian icons.

113. **St John the Baptist.** Late
15th century. Paint on panel (egg yolk
and linseed). 12½ × 9 in.
(32 × 23·5 cm.). Louvre, Paris. This
Greek icon shows St John preaching in
the desert protected by the hand of God.
The text he carries expresses his
teaching, 'Repent ye, for the kingdom
of heaven is at hand' (Matthew III.2).
The dramatic nature of the character and
the wild scenery marks the style of the
time of the Palaeologue revival. The
emaciated figure and the arrangement of
the robes recall the figures in the wall-
paintings at Mistra.

114 (above left). **The Entombment.** *Andrei Rublev.* Late
14th century–15th century. Paint on panel (yolk of egg and
linseed). The Tretyakov Gallery, Moscow. The rich colours of
this tragic scene and the expressive gestures of the mourning
women and apostles are an indication of the realism which was
to develop in the icons of the 15th century. Andrei Rublev was
the greatest master of Russian icon painting; there is a softness
and luminosity in his colours which was later to be imitated for
many years.

115 (above right). **Mosaic icon** (detail). Early 14th century.
h. 10⅝ in. (28 cm.). Opera del Duomo, Florence. The scenes on
the miniature diptych illustrate the Twelve Feasts of the Church.
The four illustrated are the *Entry into Jerusalem*, the *Crucifixion*,
the *Anastasis* or *Descent into Limbo*, and the *Ascension*. On the same
leaf are the *Pentecost* and the *Dormition of the Virgin*, whereas on
the other side are six scenes from Christ's early life.

116 (right). **The Annunciation.** Early 14th century. Mosaic.
5¼ × 3¼ in. (13 × 8 cm.). Victoria and Albert Museum,
London. One of the loveliest of the miniature Byzantine icons is
this tiny example of the *Annunciation*. It recalls the wall-
mosaics in Kahrie Cami in its expressive feeling, the
elongated figures and the architectural details of the
background. Originally supposed to be of an earlier date
because of their precious nature, such icons have nonetheless
been attributed to the time of the Palaeologue revival because of
their style.

your work. I would ask you not to forget that Byzantine civilisation lies at the roots of Russian civilisation.'

These words are an indication of the importance that the adoption by the Slav peoples of Orthodox Christianity, still has today and the imperial concepts of power and administration and, finally, Byzantine art. It is an astonishing development which has continued right up to our own time, bringing with it, in spite of so many centuries of history and profound change, the forms of thought, piety and artistic expression that originated in Byzantium between the 6th and the 12th centuries. The taking of Constantinople by the Crusaders in 1204 seemed to have extinguished that light: we have seen that even during this eclipse, new centres of light were set up in Crete, at Trebizond, and also in Macedonia, Serbia and Bulgaria. When the Palaeologues had taken up the torch, the influence of the metropolis was to be felt again even among the most staunchly independent peoples. And after the arrival of the Turks in Constantinople in 1453, when the conceptions of Anthemius of Tralles and Isidorus of Miletus were to inspire the great architect Sinan to adorn the face of Constantinople with magnificent mosques, the Slavs continued to live from the past. With time, forms developed, the iconography altered slightly and other influences intervened. But there was no break. The albums recently published in the Soviet Union on the icons and paintings of Andrei Rublev and other Russian painters of the 14th and subsequent centuries are sufficient proof of this.

SERBIA

The geographical boundaries of the Christian art of the East are, in fact, those of the Orthodox Church itself. Within Yugoslavia, one can trace the boundaries of the areas of influence of the Roman and Byzantine missions by the form of the churches—on the one hand basilicas and on the other churches with domes—and by the character of the painted decoration. This is the result of the confrontation of the Greek evangelistic activity of Cyril and Methodius with the efforts of the Roman papacy and Aquileia.

84 During the first period Serbia and Macedonia were Byzantine provinces close to Constantinople and also to Salonika, which, throughout the history of Byzantium, was a very influential artistic centre. Very few paintings of this period—prior to the end of the 12th century—have been discovered. But our knowledge was increased by the

discovery under plaster of the frescoes of Ochrid and Nerezi in Macedonia. In the charming little church at **85** Nerezi (1164), which is so Greek in appearance with its five domes and high drum, the traditional iconography suddenly takes on a striking emotional power. The Deposition, has a new dramatic aspect in the freedom of **85** movement. The entombment is equally dramatic—with the faces of the Virgin and St John twisted by suffering and even those of the angels flying in the sky. It is possible to believe that this is the work of a painter from Constantinople and that this sudden sensibility and the perfection of style owe a great deal to the new dramatic environment in which Byzantine piety found itself. Yet at Sta Sophia in Ochrid there were paintings dating from 1056—a hundred years older. Beside traditional works, there are also scenes in which the faces suddenly reveal an attempt at expression, a certain painful tension—more crudely executed, it is true, but one which heralds the astonishing success at Nerezi.

In Serbia the two churches of this period with the finest paintings are those at Milesevo and Sopocani. They date from a time when Constantinople was under Frankish domination—and one wonders if the artists escaping from the conquered capital did not set up there some of their studios.

The paintings at Milesevo date from about 1235. They include a fine portrait that definitely resembles the donor, King Vladislav, who reigned from 1230 to 1237. We know the names of three of the painters, and this division of the work probably explains the differences of style between the different parts of the church. Even within a single scene— the Resurrection, for example—one is struck by the reticence of the Holy Women, the classical grandeur of the angel, impassive and dressed in fine, slightly stylised white draperies, and the confused mass of sleeping soldiers that form a kind of base to the picture. The Virgin of the Annunciation, on the other hand, is quite untraditional and receives her celestial visitor graciously and with becoming reserve.

At Sopocani in about 1265, during the reign of King Urosh, there appeared multi-figured compositions, which invaded almost all the traditional schemes: for example, **86** the Descent into Limbo, with its crowd of resurrected figures, or the Dormition of the Virgin, with a gathering of priests and a large bodyguard of angels. At the same time the head of Christ more sorrowful at the death of his mother than happy to give her soul to the angels, bends tenderly towards his shoulder.

The movement was to continue—at Prizren, Studenica, Gracanica, Decani and, once again, at Ochrid, in the church of St Mary Peribleptos (now St Clement's), throughout the 13th and 14th centuries up to the 15th century, with a boldness of composition, complicated architectural backgrounds, firmer design, but occasionally, in the usual scenes, faces suddenly enlivened by sorrow or ecstasy.

The painters working in the churches are now Slavs, like those, for example, working for King Miliutin at the end of

117 (opposite). **The Annunciation.** Early 14th century. 36¼ × 26¾ in. (92 × 68 cm.). Macedonian State Collections, Skopje, Macedonia. Although this double-sided icon is from the Church of St Clement at Ochrid, it is probably the work of a master from Constantinople. A processional icon, it would be carried on a pole. The other side shows the *Virgin and Child*, but the graceful beauty of this *Annunciation* has made it one of the most famous of Byzantine paintings. The traditional reserve in the expression of feeling is maintained here, but other icons (plate 116), while keeping the same composition are imbued with a new emotion.

85. **The Communion of the Apostles.**
1164. Paint on plaster. Church of
St Nicholas, Nerezi, Macedonia. The
fresco extends round the apse, showing
the angels in the centre with the liturgical
fans, *ripidia*, fanning the sacraments.
Christ shown twice, according to the
traditional iconography, is distributing
the bread and wine to the Apostles. The
drapery and the expression on their faces
is particularly dramatic.

86 (left). **Jesus with the Elders.** 1265.
Paint on plaster. Sopocani, Serbia. The
Virgin and Joseph find Christ sitting in
the centre of a *synthronon* among the elders
questioning him. He is already giving the
sign of the blessing. The perspective of the
architectural elements is particularly
noteworthy.

the 13th century. Certain scenes take on a new, sometimes
very moving intensity, which enhances their religious
value.

At a time when the Turkish invasion was advancing, a
last series of paintings, in the valley of the Morava, returned to elongated, slender, elegant, somewhat precious
figures, grouped in front of complicated architectural backgrounds. Professor Talbot Rice has remarked on the contrast between the terrible military situation and this art of
charm and refuses to see this as a sign of decadence:
'Gentleness is a Christian virtue.'

BULGARIA

In Bulgaria the situation was rather different: the Bulgarians of Asparukh—Turko-Tartars—had settled in
Dobroudja, with the assent of the Basileus Constantine II,
since the middle of the 7th century. At the expense of the
Avars, they had considerably extended their territory and
merged with the Slav population. In 870, King Boris was
baptised and received into the Greek Church: his god-
father was the emperor, Michael III; and he gave permis-
sion for the disciples of Methodius to evangelise the country in the Slav dialect. The elements of the Bulgarian

civilisation were now united. Unfortunately few documents
from this period have survived. But the ceramics of Pat-
leina, particularly an astonishing portrait of St Theodorus,
painted before firing on to a series of tiles, are evidence of
the presence of techniques borrowed from Iranian art.

It was the second Bulgarian kingdom, which, after 1185
was to develop its own school of painting under Byzantine
influence: the form of the brick churches and the extent and
composition of the cycles of pictures show the connections
with the metropolis, which no doubt sent artists with its
missionaries, or trained Bulgarian artists itself. The capital
of the kingdom was at Tirnovo, where in the 13th and especially the 14th centuries, there developed a school in which
the Byzantine predominance did not prevent the expression of original temperaments.

The frescoes at Boiana, a small town near Tirnovo, date *87*
from 1259. They were painted at the instigation of the
'Sevastocrator' Kaloian, who was represented, with his **89**
wife, the 'Sevastocratissa' Desislava, in magnificent portraits in which the very human serenity of the faces contrasts with the splendour and stiffness of the costumes. The
young woman, who is smiling slightly, has a very real
grace which contrasts with the great, but imaginary beauty

87. **The church of Boiana.** 11th and 13th centuries. Bulgaria. The three parts of the church were built at various times. The original church dedicated to St Nicholas is the easternmost part, the apse of which can be seen here. The central portion was built in 1259 by the Sevastocrator Kaloian and has two storeys. In plate 86 he is seen presenting his church with his wife by his side. The annex was added in the 19th century.

of the other figures in the paintings. There are a great many of these figures, for example the saints like St Stephen, St Lawrence and St Ephraem which are more personal, more individual than usual, or those mingled in scenes, as in the bustling anxious group of doctors around Christ.

86, 87, 88   But one is struck most of all by the representations of Christ himself; first, Christ as a child, then Christ teaching, finally, the formidable Christ in triumph of the Transfiguration. It has needed little more than a hardening of the shadows, a shift of colour for the expression to be re-created anew. Later, Bulgarian painting developed in two directions. In the middle of the 14th century, the frescoes at Ivanovo are executed with great flexibility, virtuosity and vibrant colours. At almost the same time, at Zemen, a more popular art led on the other hand to the development of a drawing that was emphatic, even abrupt, but expressive and spontaneous, as in the astonishing group of the apostles sleeping in Gethsemane as Christ prays.

The existence of these two currents in Bulgarian painting is sufficient proof, it seems, that it was in no way an unquestioning copy of the art of Byzantium, but an art in which different traditions and temperaments confronted each other and intermingled to form a quite individual school.

THE RUSSIANS

Farther east, the Slavs became once more a collection of unorganised tribes after the collapse of the Avars who had dominated them: Normans from Scandinavia—the Russians whom the Byzantines called Varangians—who had arrived in this region by following the trading routes, established a state at Kiev and reigned there from 862 to 957. The successors of Rurik, Oleg, Igor and Olga have Slav names, but seem nonetheless to have been Russians. It was they who, during the 10th and 11th centuries, attacked Byzantium, signed trading treaties and were converted to Christianity. As early as 880, the patriarch Photius had tried to convert them, but it was only in 957, at Byzantium, that Queen Olga was baptised; in 989, her successor Vladimir was to marry the sister of the emperor, Basil II, and impose Christianity on his people.

Again it is not surprising that the religious art of Kiev should, from the very beginning, appear Byzantine. The

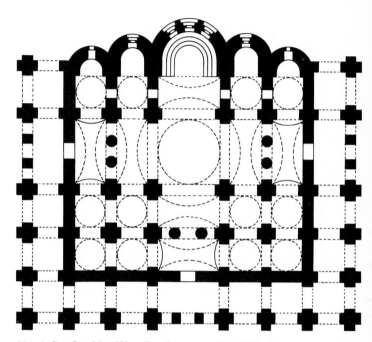

88*a*, *b*. **Sta Sophia,** Kiev, Russia. 1037–46. *(a)* The basic cross-in-square plan of the church was successively enlarged by two aisles running round the three sides from the eastern apses. *(b)* The number of domes was thus increased, and their height and shape are characteristically Russian.

88a,b Church of Sta Sophia in Kiev was founded by Prince Yaroslav about 1037 and consecrated between 1042 and 1049 by Metropolitan Theopemptes: it was a metropolitan cathedral, intended to play the same role as the other H. Sophia in Constantinople. Several times it was destroyed, restored, enlarged, abandoned and rebuilt. Recent research has reconstructed a detailed history of the church and discovered new sections of its decoration.

The original nucleus of the church is a fairly small dome at the intersection of a nave and transept of equal length. The barrel-vaults of the transept are supported by arches, which correspond to secondary naves that are also vaulted, or by apses of which there seem to have been five at the beginning. An outer aisle was built which ran round three sides of the building. This also ended in apses, and was later incorporated into the building itself. A second, wider aisle, with asymmetrical towers was then added. So in the *88a* end the building had nine naves, nine apses and seven domes—a kind of progressive dilatation of a plan based on the inscribed cross. It is a good indication of the development that Byzantine plans were later to undergo in Russia.

The interior decoration consists of mosaics and frescoes, in what might be called a simplified Byzantine style. There is the Christ Pantocrator in the dome, above the severely drawn archangels, with evangelists on pendentives. In the apse is a Virgin, standing in the attitude of an *orans*, which is also treated in a simple rather ungraceful manner. Below is a scene representing the Communion of the apostles according to the ancient iconography with six apostles coming from each side. The mosaicist was careful to maintain the individuality of the faces, which are treated simply, but this time with a certain attempt at expression. The same scene had been represented in another 11th-century church in Kiev, St Michael's, with quite different effects in the grouping of the figures, less boldness and less feeling.

Below is a traditional row of saints; and saints were also used to decorate, this time in fresco, the other parts of the building. They are depicted frontally, with great attention to individuality, which is less successful, it seems, than at Boiana. There are also scenes, particularly of episodes in the life of the Virgin, including a very beautiful, very sensitive bethrothal scene. Other frescoes, representing Prince Yarislav and his family, are in very poor condition.

In the south-west tower one moves to profane scenes—bear-hunting and squirrel-hunting with bow and arrow—that are reminiscent of the classical *venationes;* moreover the hippodrome with its royal enclosure is also shown. In other scenes, there are wrestlers, musicians, animals—even a camel. These obviously derive from the palace at Constantinople.

It is the miracle of Byzantine art that, without a break, it could become the art of the Slav peoples. This miracle must be attributed to the Orthodox Church—the Greek church of Constantinople. It is also due to the prestige of the city of Constantinople itself, which epitomised civilisation throughout the Middle Ages—as much for the Arabs and Bulgarians, who were intent on conquering it, as for the Franks, who succeeded in doing so—and whose amazement on seeing the city was so well conveyed by Villehardouin. With the travels of Cosmas Indicopleustes from the time of Justinian this glory had extended as far as Ethiopia, and thence to Ceylon. Venice, wishing to share its beauty, imitated it. Just as ancient Rome had attracted the Barbarians, so the new Rome fascinated them—and they came seeking wealth and culture.

What they found was a religion—a faith, rites, a hierarchy and churches. This religion provided a framework for daily life, it ruled people's minds and hearts, it determined the rhythm of the day's activities, it offered to all the luxury of its buildings and its ceremonies. But this religion was that of the enemy; and for a long time the peoples around Byzantium refused to embrace it—the imperial religion might be a means to enslavement. So in the 5th and 6th centuries it was the heretics—monks exiled by the Church councils or fleeing from the imperial police—who made converts. These were harmless enough people in the eyes of the Barbarians who received them because they were cut off from the imperial power. Thus the Goths became Arians, the Mesopotamians Nestorians and the Ethiopians Monophysites. Art followed soon after.

But in Europe, Orthodoxy was to do even more. What the Goth, Ulfilas, who had been converted to Arianism in Constantinople, had done for his people—the creation of a written form for their language so that they could read the Bible—Cyril and Methodius were to do for the Slavs. In order to reach believers who did not speak Greek, the Orthodox Church had to learn to speak the vernacular and translate the sacred texts into Slav, or into whatever other language was spoken by the peoples converted by its missionaries. Of course, the kings and chiefs came to Constantinople to be baptised—in Greek—or were baptised in their own capitals by Greek missionaries sent by the patriarch. But the use of the Slav language soon led to the formation of a Slav-speaking clergy, of a national clergy—which, in turn, led to the formation of national churches, to secession. It looked as if the Orthodox Church was breaking up. But only apparently so, for the faith remained the same, the liturgies were unaltered and the art of the churches remained faithful to traditions. Beyond the linguistic break a spiritual unity, which was expressed in an aesthetic unity, was preserved.

Whether the works are icons, mosaics or frescoes, they retain first of all their iconographical themes: for example, there is a long line of descent from the *Virgin of Vladimir*, an **112** icon painted in Constantinople at the beginning of the 12th century and transported to Russia which is to be found in the 14th century under the name of the 'Mother of God of the Don', in the paintings attributed to Andrei Rublev and even later. Similarly, the same type of Christ, at once noble and gentle, continues unchanged from icon to icon well into the 16th century. The iconography of stories from the life of Christ is repeated sufficiently closely

89. **Christ the Healer.** *c.* 1310. Mosaic. Kahrie Cami, Constantinople. This striking example of a miracle scene shows the familiar grouping of Christ with his apostles to the left and the object of the miracle to the right. The interior of the church is decorated with scenes from the life of the Virgin and the life of Christ.

90. **Kahrie Cami** (Chora church). 1300. Constantinople. The church itself is only a square covered by a dome but it has in front of it two narthexes and is flanked by a side-chapel.

for it to be possible in each case to find an original in the Byzantine repertoire. The saints and secular notables, shown frontally or almost frontally, retain their simplified cloaks or their stiff *chlamydes*. The angels run with the same movement and their cloaks always fall in the same folds over their tunics. The expression of the faces remains the same—whether ascetic old men with curly beards, bald Fathers of the Church with high-domed foreheads or fine-featured angels, with inclined heads and tight curls—it is the same humanity, animated by the same spirituality. Of course, new themes did arise, or rather new versions of the old themes, as in the meal of the three angels, which was probably derived from the *philoxenia* of Abraham, and which became a symbol of the Trinity. This same tableau was to be treated by Andrei Rublev in a discreetly beautiful masterpiece.

While in the West Byzantine influence was to fade and disappear, swept away by profound revolutions like the appearance of Romanesque art, Gothic art or the classical art of the Renaissance, the Orthodox church remained faithful to the old traditions. It was within these bounds that, throughout the Greek and Slav worlds, especially in Russian art, individuals had to express a new religious sensibility, a new search for beauty.

THE PALAEOLOGUES: THE LAST REVIVAL

Before leaving Byzantine art, we should return to Constantinople. Michael Palaeologus, who was at Nicaea, and who seized power at the death of Theodorus II Lascaris, succeeded, with the help of the Genoese, in driving the Franks from Constantinople (1261) and founding a dynasty that proved strong enough to resist all attacks until the fall of 1453. From the beginning, it was a much smaller empire than before, with the Seljuks in Anatolia, the Armenians in Cilicia, the Bulgarians and Serbs independent in the Balkans, while the empire of Trebizond and the Despotate of Epirus maintained their independence and the Peloponnese, despite the conquest of a few citadels,

remained in the hands of the Franks. During this difficult period, Byzantine painting was to revive once more, first in Constantinople, then in the empire itself, in particular in its Peloponnesian citadel of Mistra.

90   The church of the Saviour at Chora, now Kahrie Cami, has a whole cycle of mosaics dating from the beginning of the 14th century. The church is very small—82 feet by 82 feet, in all, or without the additions 27 feet 6 inches. The walls are entirely covered with astonishingly animated *92* mosaics recounting the lives of the Virgin and of Christ and adding to the traditional episodes allusions to hymns that had just been introduced into the liturgy. The scenes take on a new development thanks to the attention paid to the details of the event, the subsidiary characters, the decorative background and the accessories. The mosaic of the *91* Birth of the Virgin becomes the occasion for a great scene with serving women carrying torches and preparing food for the mother while the midwives stand in a corner preparing the bath for the new-born child under the indiscreet eye of the father peeping from a doorway.

    The apocryphal Gospel of St James supplied other picturesque and moving motifs like the Annunciation to Elizabeth, or the scene in which the Virgin is learning to walk and stumbles towards her mother. In the life of Christ the Gospel accounts of his childhood are interpreted in a similar way as in the census of Quirinus, in which Joseph presents his wife to the governor and registrar, or again the Flight into Egypt, preceded by Joseph's premonitory *89* dream. Christ's miracles also allow the arrangement of a picturesque group of beggars and cripples opposite the majestic, somewhat aloof apostles. It represents, in fact, a quite new vitality in the portrayal of the Gospel stories.

    Opposite these pictures, which were in the narthex, in an *90* arcade of the exonarthex, is the Christ Emmanuel which remains majestic and impassive. In the apse of the side chapel which is decorated with frescoes, the Anastasis, *93* here too represented by Christ's descent into Limbo, takes on a new dramatic power in its extension onto the sides of this apse.

    Overhead extends a representation of the Last Judgement, in which Christ is enthroned, surrounded by a *synthronon* of apostles and a host of angels standing over the tiny figures of the damned. And in the mosaic dedication scenes, one with Theodorus Metochetes, the founder of the church, the other with Prince Isaac Porphyrogenetes and his sister Maria at his feet, the Christ, accompanied on the second occasion by a Virgin of intercession, has the same solemn majesty that was present everywhere in the previous period. Nevertheless the humanity of the group scenes is a new departure and shows that once more Byzantine art was trying to revitalise its conventions with more daring than ever before.

    This is to be found with even greater freedom in the frescoes of the churches of Mistra in the Peloponnese. In the 14th century the city was dependent on Constantinople; it was governed by one of the emperor's sons, who

91. **The Ascension.** Paint on plaster. Pantanassa church, Mistra, Peloponnese, Greece. The frescoes of the vault of the sanctuary include this beautiful detail of the Ascension. The grace and realism of the expressions and the draperies are quite outstanding (see plate 96). The Virgin, and here the Apostles, stand among the trees, witnessing the miracle of the Ascension depicted on the vault.

brought with him the latest artistic inspiration from the capital, which itself was enjoying a really intellectual life. In spite of its connections with western culture—it was surrounded by Frankish principalities and several of its princes had married Italian princesses—it was very little affected in its architecture and decoration by foreign influences. The architecture is Byzantine and the painting was dependent on Constantinople.   *95*

    There is a whole series of churches here all decorated between 1290 and 1430, although they show there was a gradual development of style. In the oldest, that of St Demetrius, the Virgin stands in the apse, as at Nicaea, above the Communion of the Apostles, and the style is somewhat cold and official. But the compositions suddenly free themselves from the confines of the 13th and 14th centuries and develop on several levels at once, in dramatic landscapes or on architecturally complicated stairs. The figures, whose physical characteristics are emphasised and whose costumes are ablaze with colour, bustle about these operatic settings, as if afraid of becoming lost in them, for example in the church of the Peribleptos.

    At the Pantanassa, Christ walks at the head of a crowd   *94* through a gorge enclosed by rocks to Lazarus's tomb, the door of which opens into the cliff face. Behind, the Pharisees, hidden up to the knees stand watching. Some men have just taken off the pink marble door, Lazarus rises in his bandages preceded by a friend, who is still holding his nose in his scarf. A gap in the surface of the painting deprives us of the two prostrated sisters. This is a grandiose, dramatic, and very impressive *mise-en-scène*.

    The vaults of the Peribleptos lead straight to the sky: in   *96* the apse, the Virgin receives the homage of the angels; under the preceding arch is the Ascension, in which the mandorla of Christ giving his blessing is carried by four hovering angels above the Virgin and the Apostles who

92. **The monastery of Lavra,** on Mount Athos. Greece. 903. The whole complex of the fortified monastery is seen here from the south-west. The history of the buildings is complicated, but the fortifications can be clearly seen, as can the domes of the Katholikon, the main church in the centre.

stand gesticulating in a landscape of blossoming trees. This is followed by the entry into Jerusalem with a colourful crowd of spectators jostling in front of the multi-storeyed buildings. In the dome is a Christ Pantocrator in a medallion above the Apostles sitting in a circle. In the other arms of the cross, the Nativity, the Baptism, the Transfiguration and the Descent of the Holy Ghost on the Apostles are treated with the same joyful exuberance.

A good way of appreciating this transformation in Byzantine painting is by means of a theatrical comparison. Usually the figures are traditionally placed on a narrow stage, before a plain wall. The acting is solemn and conventional. The scene is set by the arrangement of a few 'props' on the stage. In the 13th century, the plain backdrop is replaced by changing backdrops depicting various, complicated architectural scenes; but the characters remain isolated from these settings by a wall that confines them to their narrow platform and which enables them to stand out against a plain, bright surface. In the 14th century, the backdrop is replaced by 'flats'. The wall is broken and arranged at various depths; the stage becomes deeper and is filled up. The actors, too, are placed at different depths, separated by architectural elements or by rocks in country scenes. At the same time the actors move and gesticulate more freely and the 'walkers-on', until then a few figures standing motionless at the sides of the stage, now increase in number and take a more animated part in the action. The two-dimensional surface has been broken. The action now unfolds within complex, clashing structures, with contradictory perspectives: this may not be western space, organised in perspective, but it is space.

As can be seen we are now a long way from the definition with which we began. It would be interesting to take the comparison further, to study side by side, page by page, the simultaneous achievements of painters in the East and in the West, beginning with Giotto and the mosaicist of Kahrie Cami. The great collections of works on the history of art are forced to preserve geographical as well as chronological classifications. But it would be intriguing to see what place would be occupied by the painters of Mistra if they were suddenly confronted in the same book with their contemporaries in Siena, Florence or Padua. It is likely that they would appear as free, as imaginative, and as profoundly human.

The life-span of this Byzantine art was to be prolonged well beyond the revolution of the time of the Palaeologues. This is not only because it had laid down the principles to which the religious art of the Slavs was to continue to adhere; but also because in the region of Constantinople itself, even during the vicissitudes of the Turkish conquest, the monasteries acted as conservatories in which the works of the past were piously preserved and where new works continued to be produced according to the unchanging formulas. The most famous of all these monasteries were those on Mount Athos. On the Holy mountain, isolated in their peninsula, the monasteries increased in number, at least from the 9th century. Separated from each other, enclosed within their walls, each community had several churches of its own. There were, as at Vatopedi and Chilandari, groups of traditional paintings. The *iconostases* kept their icons, often repainted, unfortunately, and the libraries preserved precious manuscripts, Gospel-books, psalters, prayer-books and devotional works of various kinds. In this way the religious world of Byzantium has survived to our own day in the popular form of monasticism.

Church Treasures

COURT ART

It is obviously the theocratic nature of the Byzantine empire, the fundamental union of theology and politics, which makes it necessary to devote a chapter to Byzantine luxury in a book on Christian art. There are other periods in history when the sovereign, not content simply to encourage artists and craftsmen by giving them the work of decorating his palace and chapels, also founded studios and workshops, decreed monopolies and centred around his own person the entire labours of the luxury industries of his time. We have only to think of Louis XIV or George IV. It comes as no surprise therefore to learn that the *basileis* forbade anyone else to use silk and purple, organised the cultivation of mulberry-bushes and the breeding of silkworms imported from China, monopolised the crushing of murex to produce the purple dye, in Phoenicia and elsewhere, and made these sumptuous fabrics the very sign of their grandeur: the Porphyrogenetes, those born in the purple, were the members of the imperial family; and one had to be a very high functionary indeed to enjoy the privilege of mixing the wool of one's cloak with a few threads of silk. The rich brocades that were to be found in the tombs of the kings and saints of East and West bear the mark of their origin in the imperial workshops of Constantinople.

It is easy to understand, too, why enlightened emperors should have encouraged the copying of manuscripts, and that there were produced for them and around them volumes of supreme quality. In all our libraries, the most famous manuscripts preserved today in London, Paris, Rome, Venice, Moscow or on Mount Sinai, bear the name and even the image of the emperor for whom they were created.

An industry like that of ivory carving has always been reserved, if only because of the price of its products, for gods and kings. We have only to think of the bed made by the Phoenicians for Azarael, the king of Damascus, and which was discovered in the excavations at Aslan Tash—where it was taken by a conquering Hittite—or of the chryselephantine statues of Phidias, the Pallas in Athens and the Zeus at Olympia. The production of the imperial workshops was so prolific that examples or imitations of it are to be found in all the museums of Europe and America.

Masterpieces of precious metalwork and jewellery, too, are intended only for the very rich. The gold and silver work, the inlaying of precious stones and the enamelling of the Byzantine period created objects of unequalled richness and of a rarely attained perfection. Again it is the splendour of the court at Constantinople that shines through the decoration of its ceremonies, the brilliance that enveloped both men and things.

It is, therefore, a courtly art. It is also an affirmation of power and the revelation of fantastic wealth.

94. The Gospel of St John (above). 8th century. Vellum. 12 × 8⅞ in. (30 × 22·5 cm.). Library of the Divinity School, Duke University, North Carolina. This detail is typical of the borders and decorative initials of a Byzantine manuscript.

93. Epitaphios from Salonika (opposite). Embroidered silk. Byzantine Museum, Athens. The central panel shows Christ mourned by angels; to the left and right are two scenes from the Communion of the Apostles and the border is a series of greek crosses in medallions.

95. Byzantine silk. 8th century. Sens cathedral, France. The shroud of St Victor, this silk shows the motif of the lion strangler, descended from a distant Mesopotamian origin. Translated into Christian themes the *Gilgamesh* hero became identified with Samson. The decorative effect is most striking in this instance.

But this courtly art is also a Christian art. The rich fabrics were intended not only for palaces but also for churches; they clothed not only emperors but also patriarchs and shrouded the corpses not only of princes but of saints. The manuscripts written out and painted in the imperial studios were holy scriptures or collections of homilies by St John Chrysostom or St Gregory of Nazianzus. The ivories are reliquaries as well as toilet articles— and in both cases are decorated with pictures of saints or pious scenes, so much so that the few caskets that are decorated with pictures of horsemen and wild animals may be dated from the iconoclastic period. The goldwork is now preserved in church treasuries, but in most cases it was for the Church that it was created in the first place—golden chalices and onyx patens, enamelled reliquaries and pectoral crosses glittering with stones. The emperor put the luxury of a refined civilisation at the service of the faith, and of the Church.

Moreover, this luxury in objects merely added one final note to the astonishing concert of colours of a Byzantine church. The shining mosaic domes are gigantic pieces of goldwork; the saints stand along the apse as they do around a vase; the iconostasis is perhaps less impressive only than the Pala d'Oro, and its icons less gilded than enamels. The Christ and the Virgin in the domes are dressed like emperors, the angels like high dignitaries or soldiers of the imperial guard. And the liturgy that takes place in the nave and choir is reminiscent of the splendour of imperial ceremonies.

The unity of Byzantine civilisation springs from this identity.

TEXTILES

The ancient history of textiles has been confused because of their fragility. We have abundant information about Egyptian Coptic fabrics—for which, like the papyri, the dry climate and the sand provided exceptionally good conditions for preservation. Except for a few discoveries in the Syrian desert, where fragments were found in the tombs at Palmyra or in a tower at Halabiye on the Euphrates, as far as antiquity is concerned we are limited to the very inadequate evidence of illustrated documents which give the forms or the colours, but give no indication of the materials or weaving methods. In the case of the Byzantine textiles, at least the more luxurious of the silks, we can judge from actual examples: those in museums or church treasuries come from tombs or sarcophagi that were sufficiently well sealed to have preserved them for centuries.

Many of the Coptic materials that have come down to us belong to Christian art. They follow directly on those that had treated pagan or merely decorative motifs— though these also continued to be popular. The Coptic materials were either tapestries, worked in wool on linen backing, or embroideries. Mixed with the wool one finds silk or even metal thread—gold thread. And sometimes the material is cotton.

Tapestry is like mosaic: one can either follow or refuse to accept the technique. There are therefore cases when the imitation of Hellenistic painting can be quite astonishing in its effects of light and shade. But elsewhere one notices the arrival of motifs that are definitely of Sassanian origin. Some of these emerged, in the reign of Justinian, in the mosaics at Antioch: carpets of flowers, winged ibexes, garlanded lions. They are to be found again in Coptic art, thus starting a line of development that was to pass through the whole of Byzantine art: horsemen, whose horses adopt the 'flying gallop', rear legs outstretched, and hunters of wild animals, were easy enough to transform into saints—St Michael, in particular, or St George. The pattern inscribed within a circle or a square, and often repeated or reversed becomes as much a decorative motif as the elephants or griffons, which do not seem to have taken on a symbolic character on their arrival in a Christian environment.

110, *95*   The Byzantine textiles from the imperial workshops were, above all, silks with repeated motifs, often very large and often influenced by Iranian traditions, as in the great silk eagles found in the sarcophagus of the bishop St Germain at Auxerre, or the elephants of Charlemagne's shroud at Aachen. These are purple silks, in which the motif is worked in gold thread. Many silks depict figures of religious origin like the one preserved in the Vatican, which is of the 7th century and has medallions showing, against a red background, scenes from the life of the Virgin—the Annunciation and the Nativity. Or again, on the fine silk formerly in the Kaiser-Friedrich Museum in Berlin, the primitive theme of the prophet Daniel in the lions' den, surrounded by the other saints, has a particularly eastern quality in the splendour of their costumes, while the rows of small churches, all alike, round the border are reminiscent of Antioch, the Syrian capital. The same materials are to be found in illustrated documents, worn by both saints and emperors, angels and Christ. Thus the dignitaries, who, in the course of ceremonies walked in procession past the mosaic figures in the palaces and churches, were clad in equally sumptuous materials which caught the light in the same way as the mosaics. The em-

42,43   press's attendants wear clothes decorated with geometrical or floral motifs, and Theodora's state cloak has an embroidered panel depicting the Adoration of the Magi.

A number of fabrics or richly embroidered liturgical vestments, usually of later periods, have also survived. As I have already said, there are Coptic iconographical materials. These may have been used by the clergy for services; embroidery allows for the most complex scenes to be transferred on to materials—on any scale required. Here again the imperial and Christian liturgies come together: if it is an emperor who is glorified on a famous silk of the 10th century, in Bamberg cathedral, it is the entombment

93   of Christ that is depicted on the *epitaphios* at Salonica—with a relief and a richness that enable this shroud to give a quality of triumph even to the mourning of Good Friday.

96. **Chancel plate from Constantinople.** 10th century. Marble. S. Marco, Venice. Byzantine decorative sculpture often has, apart from geometric motifs, stylised representations of foliage and animals arranged in a completely oriental symmetry. The border of rosettes is also found in ivories.

SCULPTURE AND IVORIES

There is no Byzantine religious sculpture. And after the first few centuries there is no imperial sculpture either. The cause of this disappearance was the fear of relapsing into idolatry. Even in ivory, there exists only one Virgin (in the Victoria and Albert Museum London) that is treated in the round—it is no more than 12 inches high and is not very different from other Virgins that are treated in high relief and backed on to plaques. Similarly, the figured sculpture of the sarcophagi, which had been the glory of early Christian art, disappeared rapidly. As a result, sculpture was almost entirely limited to capitals, chancel plates and deco- *96,97a,b* rative relief. The distinctive character of sculpted Byzantine decoration, which in renouncing the three-dimensional ends up more like wickerwork, or lace—contrasting white motifs against a black background—is often enhanced by an astonishing technical perfection. Once again the impression of wealth and luxury strikes one in the finish of the work. The capitals from the marble quarries of the *97a,b* Marmara Islands or from the workshops of the capital were often exported, often copied, and fit naturally into the architecture between the marble facings and the mosaics.

The transition is easy with the ivories, which are very numerous and very beautiful: many of the objects in this category are of surprising richness and perfection. They are usually fairly small panels—most of them being less

97a, b. **Byzantine capitals.** *(a)* The similarity of this capital from St Apollinare Nuovo in Ravenna with the one to the right is striking, but not surprising as they probably came from the same workshops. *(b)* The capitals from H. Sergius and Bacchus in Constantinople are some of the best examples of 6th century Byzantine carving, of a finely pierced pattern of stylised acanthus leaves.

than 12 inches high. The reproductions give the impression that the originals were much larger—the detail is so finely worked that it loses nothing by a change of scale. These plaques were sometimes used as icons—treated as objects of devotion and placed in iconostases. They were also used as parts of caskets, reliquaries, manuscript covers or even in furniture—as in the richly worked throne of Bishop Maximian at Ravenna (6th century).

Similar contrasts are to be found in later centuries between works that are very noble, in the restraint and hieratic quality of their composition and style, and others that are freer and more vital. The 10th-century Harbaville triptych in the Louvre shows Christ enthroned with the Virgin and the Precursor on either side of him, surrounded by five rows of saints. The perfection of the technique gives a supreme elegance to the whole work, in spite of the simplicity, not to say monotony, of the composition.

In contrast to these somewhat rigid presentations, there are also animated scenes illustrating the holy scriptures; examples can be found from every period. Attributed to the 4th century is the Trivulzio ivory which depicts the Resurrection of Christ.

A large casket with a flat lid, of the 11th or 12th century, which is now in the Cleveland Museum of Art shows an illustration of the Fall of Adam and Eve on the front in a frame composed of juxtaposed rosettes—a very common motif of the period. The figures are isolated, the drawing and relief are executed in a somewhat summary manner, but the composition of the whole is very expressive. There are scenes that are rendered in a far more dramatic way, as in the 11th-century Death of the Virgin in the Worcester Art Museum. The iconography is traditional, but the sculptor has tried much more than other artists to show the Apostles' grief in the variety of their attitudes and expressions, and to bring out the movements of Christ.

Of course the scenes illustrated on the ivories obey the general rules of iconography. But the change in technique allowed the artist to express himself better perhaps; and, very often, these pictures in low relief, enlivened nevertheless by the play of shadows take on a greater emotional value than do paintings.

GOLDSMITH'S WORK

Christian metalwork seems to have existed from a very early date. It was natural that one should wish to celebrate mass with the richest possible goblets and plates, chalices and patens. Gilt glass and glass engraved with busts of saints or narrative scenes were used, precious stones were carved, gold and silver chiselled. In the Syria of the 5th and 6th centuries a great deal of attention was paid to the liturgical utensils: chalices encrusted with precious stones were decorated with inscriptions and crosses and

98. **Byzantine ivory casket.** 11th–12th centuries.
$5\frac{1}{8} \times 18\frac{3}{4} \times 7\frac{3}{4}$ in. (*c.* 13 × 46·5 × 19·5 cm.). Cleveland
Museum of Art, Cleveland, Ohio, Gift of W. G. Mather,
F. F. Prentiss, John L. Severance and J. H. Wade. The ivory

plaques attached to the wooden casket represent scenes from
the story of Adam and Eve. The bands of rosettes are
characteristic of the period.

99. **The Death of the Virgin.** 11th century. Ivory,
$4\frac{1}{2} \times 6\frac{1}{2}$ in. (*c.* 11·5 × 16·5 cm.). Worcester Art Museum,
Worcester, Massachusetts. The carving is simple and the
iconography traditional, but the attempt to convey feeling,
especially in the group of Apostles to the right, is exceptional.
The plaque comes from a Byzantine ivory casket.

100. **David's anointing** (below left). 7th century. Silver paten
found in Cyprus. Diameter *c.* $10\frac{1}{2}$ in. (26·5 cm.). Metropolitan
Museum of Art, New York. The scene is depicted in a more complex way in the illustrations of the psalters. The background,
a colonnade with a central arch, is frequently found in this sort
of object. In front are the sacrifical altar and animals. The
classical character of this Byzantine paten is very accentuated.

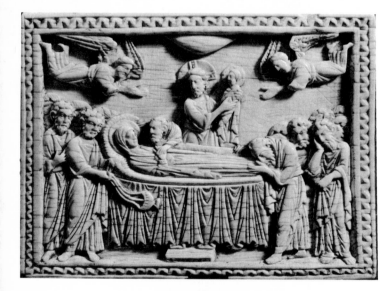

sometimes, as the metal was being chased, they were
ornamented with medallions enclosing busts of the apostles.
Special mention should be made of the Antioch chalice—
whose authenticity was so bitterly, and so vainly disputed
—in which, around a plain vase, a casing of chased silver
is covered by a scroll of vine-leaves in the volutes of which
sit Christ and the apostles. The plates were even richer in
design: a fine series has been discovered in Cyprus that
depicts episodes in the life of David. Sometimes, as in
David hunting or David and Goliath, the design evokes
bucolic scenes from Hellenistic gold objects whereas, in
the Anointing scene or David's marriage, the decoration *100*
and composition of imperial plates come to mind—as in the
famous 'Shield of Theodosius' in Madrid, for example.
More surprising, on account of the complexity of an iconography that is often to be found around the apses of
churches, are the communion plates, like the Riha paten,
on which the Communion of the Apostles receiving both
bread and wine is shown in a single scene.

The liturgy required other objects. From the 6th century there are incense burners with narrative scenes, ripidia—ceremonial fans—and reliquaries—like that representing St Simeon Stylites besieged by a serpent, of *101*
which a fragment is preserved in the Louvre.

Constantinople was to produce even richer works, first
by replacing silver with gold in chased-work, then by

adding to the gold a brilliant, multi-coloured pattern of precious stones, cameos and enamels. The cross that was planted on Golgotha was covered with precious stones. And pictures of it, which were reproduced everywhere in the decoration of churches before and particularly during the iconoclastic period, were taken up by the goldsmiths—
20, 22 it figures, for example, on the mosaics of Sta Pudenziana in Rome. It also gave rise to richly decorated altar-crosses and processional crosses. The chalices and patens gleamed and shone. They went as far as to have them carved out of hard stones—onyx or jasper—with elaborate gold mountings set off with chased or engraved motifs. Reliquaries and manuscript covers are enriched with precious stones. Through the art of *cloisonné* enamel the coloured pictures, which were so essential for the devoted, could be inserted into gold
102 backgrounds: medallions, busts and figures, where gold outlines insured both the clarity of the design and the limitation of the colours, were enclosed in gold plaques to form
105, 106 icons, retables, reliquaries and crucifixes. They are also to be found on both ecclesiastical and private jewellery. This refined technique despite its being of 'Barbarian' origin
107 produced some astonishing masterpieces: the Pala d'Oro, in the treasury of S. Marco, Venice, presents an unrivalled collection.

Goldsmith's work was eventually used in the framing of icons and even invaded the icons themselves, by replacing a background of painted gold by gold or silver *dentelle*, once again encrusted. These embellishments are regarded as being of a much later period; they became very common in the Slav countries; sometimes they contain elements of great style, which were often used again.

This taste for luxury in the decoration of the altar and of its plate reached the West through Carolingian art. In this way, the western ecclesiastical ceremonies also retained something of the splendours of the imperial court of Byzantium.

MANUSCRIPTS AND ICONS

Obviously, we must return here to the subject of manuscripts and icons, which are also objects of luxury. One experiences a curious feeling of respect when the Vatican librarian, with impressive care, hands the visitor one of the brilliant codices, in which among the columns of impec-
101, 94 cable calligraphy, beneath borders of stylised foliage enriched with fine gold threads, are illustrations as bright as enamels. Even when they are very small, nothing is missing from the complex scene represented; sometimes one can even make out the different stages of a continuous narrative. In others the image takes up the entire page and is laid out like a full-scale picture. As on the fly-leaf of the
69 collection of the Homilies of St John Chrysostom, in the Bibliothèque Nationale in Paris, the saint is handing his work to the Emperor Nicephorus Botaniates (1078–81).

Icons are usually portraits: they represent, either full-
111 length or more often as busts, Christ, the Virgin and the saints, according to certain well defined types. The

101. **Reliquary of St Simeon Stylites.** 6th century. Chased silver, traces of gilding. Louvre, Paris. The saint is shown besieged by a serpent on the top of his column.

'imaginary portrait' of Christ is as closely related to a prototype as it would have been had the artists been able to refer to an authentic original. In fact, this is just what they did do, their model being identified by its miraculous origin. When one looks at a number of icons, one sees that the pictures of Christ resemble each other even more closely than do different photographs of the same man, almost as much as different copies of the same photograph.

It is this resemblance that turned the icon into a devotional object, that conferred a presence upon it. It was the same in the case of the Virgin, either the Virgin of the Annunciation or the Virgin and Child, with the difference that painters could choose between equally authentic models ranging from the most hieratic, with Virgin and Child in the same axis, to ever more maternal and human ones. In this way one arrives at the Virgin of Vladimir, and the *112* Virgin in Russian art.

The saints also had their fixed iconography which, when the saints were also bishops, may well have been based on *113* real portraits; in fact there were enough pictures of donors on the walls of churches for prototypes to be found sometimes. Whereas the faces are often treated simply with differences between them that can only be due to the caprice of the painter, one also finds, in Macedonia, for example, pictures of St Nicholas, with white curly hair, full forehead, short, rounded beard, and a kindly expres-

102. **St Peter.** 11th century. Enamel on gold. Metropolitan Museum of Art. New York. Gift of J. Pierpont Morgan, 1917. This Byzantine medallion is one of a set from an icon of St Gabriel formerly in an old church of the monastery at Jumati in Georgia. It shows how the traditional attitude and appearance of the saint was adopted even in the difficult medium of cloisonné enamel.

103 (opposite left). **Johannes Climacus.** The Heavenly Ladder. 1082. *c.* 10½ × 8 in. (27 × 20 cm.). Princeton University Library, Princeton, U.S.A. This Byzantine guide to monastic life is decorated with extremely lively marginal illustrations, such as this heavenly ladder.

104. **Archangel** (opposite right). Andrei Rublev. 14th–15th century. Paint on panel. Tretyakov Gallery, Moskow. The angel comes from the left-hand panel of a Deesis icon, from Zvenigorod.

sion around the slightly smiling mouth: but the same face is to be found from one icon to another, and the slight differences due to different hands have far less importance than the certainty of identification.

It is of course helped by the identity of the costume. In the case of the Virgin, it is carried very far—there is the same edging to the dark veil over the forehead, the same very fine golden fringes, the robe is braided and fastened in the same way to the shoulder and there are often small embroidered crosses in the axis of the face and under the shoulders.

In more complex scenes one finds the same iconographical schemes that govern such representations in manuscripts and monumental painting. Again, there are variants, but these are due to differences between the models rather **116,117** than to the caprice of the artists. The Annunciation, for example, is often represented either on a single panel or on two identical panels intended, perhaps, to form the door of an iconostasis.

The Virgin, sitting or standing in front of a seat, has her back to her house, while the angel stands out against a golden sky, having only just alighted. One can understand that the Virgin is somewhat taken aback by this celestial arrival; she drops her spindle and stretches out her right hand in a self-protective gesture.

One is always amazed at being able to offer a description, whether technical or subjective, of several pictures at once —and to be able, each time, to affirm that each of them has its own personality. Moreover, that personality is sufficiently marked for one to be able to recognise in different icons the hand of the same painter.

Lastly, there are groups of icons that present a series of interrelated pictures. Arranged either as a frame around a central picture they might relate episodes in the life of the saint represented, or they might consist of six or nine pictures grouped in a rectangle and depicting, for example, **115** the principal feasts of the Church according to the usual iconography. One finds here, with the return to small-scale

figures, the same vitality and verve as in the miniatures, sometimes, too, paradoxically enough, the scope of the monumental compositions. As in the manuscripts the scenes taken from the lives of the saints are particularly vivid; these scenes of miracles or martyrdoms allow a greater freedom and sometimes tend almost to caricature.

We should not forget that many icons are painted on both sides: they were enclosed in the frame of the iconostasis, offering the faithful the help of intercessors who would be ready to come to their aid. The piety of Orthodox Christians, who come to kiss the images, is as if justified by the gravity, nobility and spirituality of the serene figures —Christ, the Virgin, angels and saints—who receive their *104* fervour. The luxury which surrounds the artistic expression of the religious sentiments of the Byzantines doubtless proves disconcerting to some souls, but other believers must be granted their need to consecrate to the service of God their most beautiful and most precious possessions. It must be remembered that, contrary to what may have happened at other times and in other countries of the Christian world, neither the influence of Imperial art nor the luxury of so many of the accessories of the services ever harmed the dignity, the reserve or the piety of Byzantine decoration.

CONCLUSION

Once Christian art had emerged from the initial attempts of the catacomb period—apart from the brilliant flashes of the Irish miniatures—there is no doubt that it was dominated for a long period of its history by Byzantine iconography. Even when the birth of Romanesque art interrupted this domination in a vast part of the West and the East, everything continued; Byzantine iconography was repeated in time and space and the Transfiguration painted in Russia by Rublev in the 14th century was the same Transfiguration that, in the 6th century, was set in mosaic in the apse of the monastery of St Catherine on Mount **46** Sinai. The same formidable-looking Christ threatens one

from the tops of domes and, in the apses, the same grave-faced Virgin offers her intercession. Thousands of identical or similar saints and thousands of angels stand at attention along the walls, on the sides of pillars and along the bases of the domes of churches. The 'painter's book' was used everywhere in commissioning work, the details of which were copied from icons and miniatures taken from one place to another. The same interpretations of the same scenes were imposed on all artists, whether fresco-painters, mosaicists, miniaturists or ivory-workers, with as much firmness as were the dogmas of the faith. They were caught up in a system, an implacable orthodoxy. It must be admitted that the Byzantine theocracy—the close union of Church and Empire—represented a dictatorship over art that extended beyond the boundaries of the Greek Empire, and even beyond the limits of Greek Christianity.

But the reader led by the illustrations and travelling from Salonika to Venice, from Bulgaria to Cappadocia, from the Copts to the Carolingians, is hardly conscious of this. It is not that the differences escaped him: they did not affect him. All these works it is true had a single thought which was conveyed, so to speak, by a myriad of voices singing in unison. But like an actor reciting a famous poem that others have recited before him, the painter painting again a famous picture could not help but introduce his own emotion into it. At first, of course, it was not his own emotion, through the model he perceived the intentions of the first painter. But beyond this he tried to recreate the feelings that this painter had had for his characters—for the shepherds hearing the singing of the angels at the Nativity, the Doctors in the temple troubled by the intelligence of the young Jesus, the trembling apostle who prepares to drink from the chalice at the Last Supper. These are not dry conventions, but messages that can be conveyed by lines and colours as well as, even better than, by words. In the midst of these images, one is plunged into a living gospel—passed on from one artist to another.

It is not necessarily our gospel and it may, at first, seem foreign to us. The perception of Giotto, the grace of Fra Angelico and the dread of Grünewald have accustomed us to other harmonies, that perhaps move us more. But we will not escape the Byzantine expression without being affected by it. The depth of these eyes, the modesty of these lips, the freedom of movements, the flight of wings, and the brilliance of these celestial lights surely have a spiritual meaning for us. For Byzantine art is a religious art.

Perhaps we may be embarrassed by the fact that it is also an imperial art, that the costumes are often those of the court and that these works are filled with details of etiquette and seem to have an overwhelming desire for brilliance and luxury. We should beware of such an anachronism, for we are in the midst of a triumphant Christianity which is the religion of the emperor born into the purple. Nothing could be fine enough for Christ. We have only to think of the nave of Hagia Sophia.

We should also go beyond the court; after all, this imperial art, this art of grandeur, is also that of the monks of Sinai and Athos, of the Serbian peasants who came to Nerezi to hear mass, of the craftsmen of Kiev and of the Venetian merchants. In its splendour it brought to everyone an additional knowledge of God, a revelation of the relations between man and Christ, the certainty of intercession, a way to sanctity—directly, through its very presence. And this presence is not only that of St John Chrysostom, St Simeon Stylites, Jonah or Noah. It is also that of the painter, of the individual interpreter, who once again has said what was expected of him, but in his own way, through his own mastery or technical inadequacy, his enthusiasm or serenity, his joy or anxiety. Perhaps our sociological knowledge is insufficient to enable us to know how much of this was contributed by, say, the Serbian temperament or Armenian piety. Any attempts to distinguish between different schools must be based on formal criteria. And between the different painters, we can only distinguish different 'hands'. Where so much remains conjectural, each of us may delve deeper for himself.

Historical and Artistic Landmarks of the Early Christian and Byzantine World

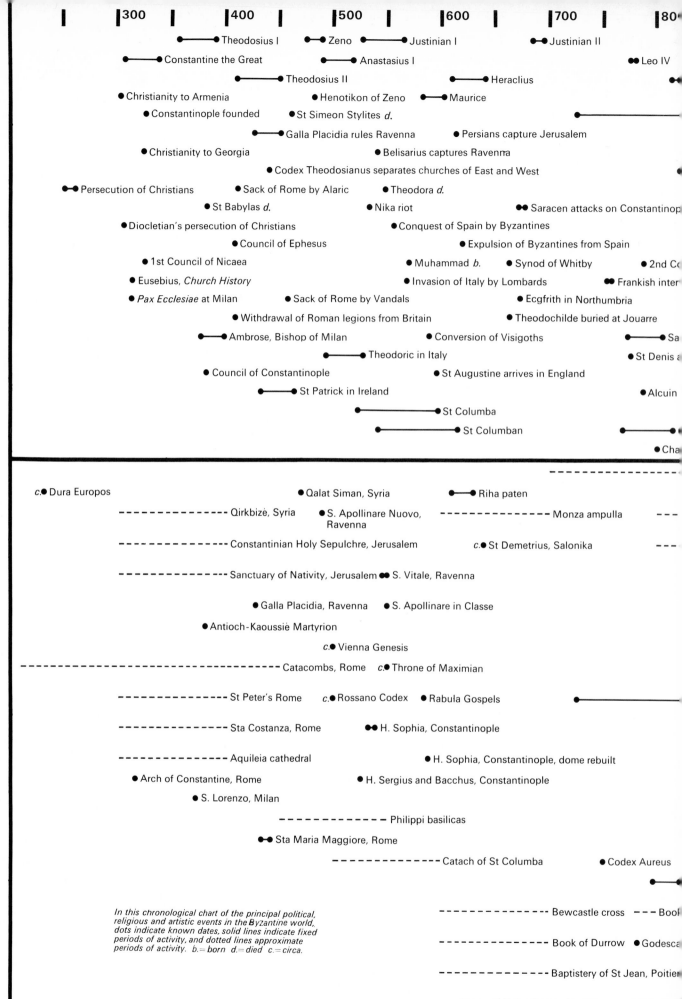

300 400 500 600 700 80

Theodosius I — Zeno — Justinian I — Justinian II
Constantine the Great — Anastasius I — Leo IV
Theodosius II — Heraclius
Christianity to Armenia — Henotikon of Zeno — Maurice
Constantinople founded — St Simeon Stylites *d.*
Galla Placidia rules Ravenna — Persians capture Jerusalem
Christianity to Georgia — Belisarius captures Ravenna
Codex Theodosianus separates churches of East and West
Persecution of Christians — Sack of Rome by Alaric — Theodora *d.*
St Babylas *d.* — Nika riot — Saracen attacks on Constantinop
Diocletian's persecution of Christians — Conquest of Spain by Byzantines
Council of Ephesus — Expulsion of Byzantines from Spain
1st Council of Nicaea — Muhammad *b.* — Synod of Whitby — 2nd Co
Eusebius, *Church History* — Invasion of Italy by Lombards — Frankish inter
Pax Ecclesiae at Milan — Sack of Rome by Vandals — Ecgfrith in Northumbria
Withdrawal of Roman legions from Britain — Theodochilde buried at Jouarre
Ambrose, Bishop of Milan — Conversion of Visigoths — Sa
Theodoric in Italy — St Denis
Council of Constantinople — St Augustine arrives in England
St Patrick in Ireland — Alcuin
St Columba
St Columban
Cha

c. Dura Europos — Qalat Siman, Syria — Riha paten
Qirkbizé, Syria — S. Apollinare Nuovo, Ravenna — Monza ampulla
Constantinian Holy Sepulchre, Jerusalem — *c.* St Demetrius, Salonika
Sanctuary of Nativity, Jerusalem — S. Vitale, Ravenna
Galla Placidia, Ravenna — S. Apollinare in Classe
Antioch-Kaoussié Martyrion
c. Vienna Genesis
Catacombs, Rome — *c.* Throne of Maximian
St Peter's Rome — *c.* Rossano Codex — Rabula Gospels
Sta Costanza, Rome — H. Sophia, Constantinople
Aquileia cathedral — H. Sophia, Constantinople, dome rebuilt
Arch of Constantine, Rome — H. Sergius and Bacchus, Constantinople
S. Lorenzo, Milan
Philippi basilicas
Sta Maria Maggiore, Rome
Catach of St Columba — Codex Aureus
Bewcastle cross — Book
Book of Durrow — Godesca
Baptistery of St Jean, Poitier
Abbey of Notre Dame, Jouarre — Palace c
c.

In this chronological chart of the principal political, religious and artistic events in the Byzantine world, dots indicate known dates, solid lines indicate fixed periods of activity, and dotted lines approximate periods of activity. b.= born d.= died c.= circa.

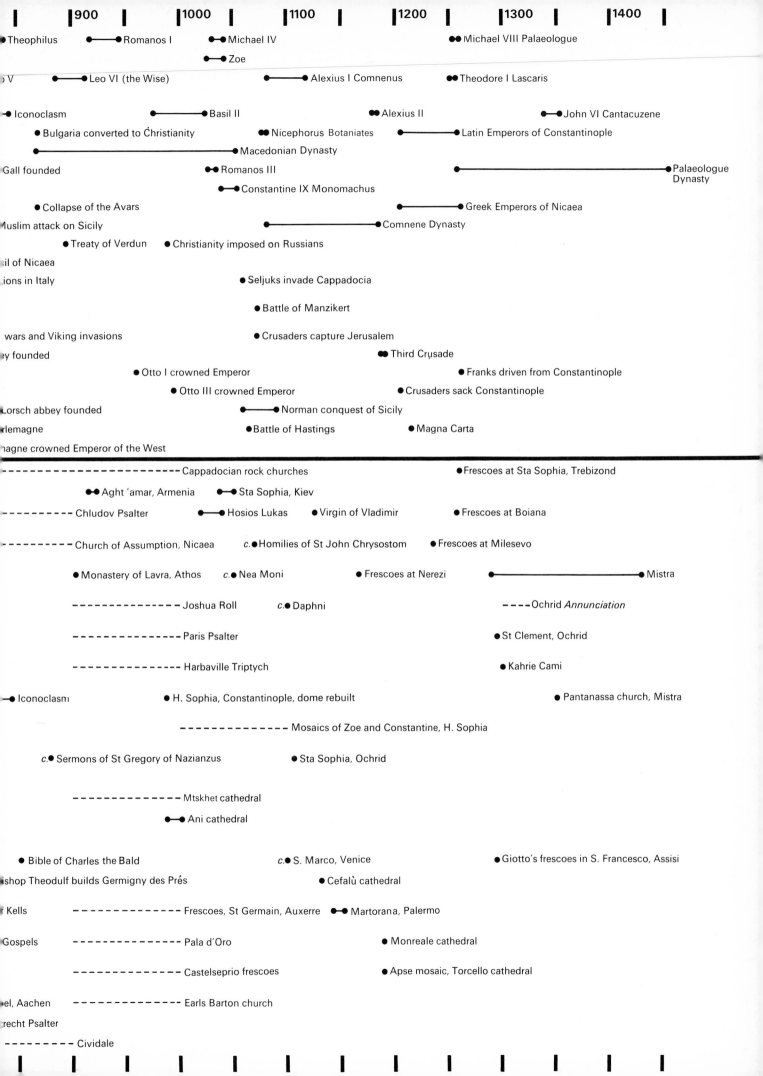

900 · 1000 · 1100 · 1200 · 1300 · 1400

- Theophilus
- Romanos I
- Michael IV
- Michael VIII Palaeologue
- Zoe
- ..V Leo VI (the Wise)
- Alexius I Comnenus
- Theodore I Lascaris
- Iconoclasm
- Basil II
- Alexius II
- John VI Cantacuzene
- Bulgaria converted to Christianity
- Nicephorus Botaniates
- Latin Emperors of Constantinople
- Macedonian Dynasty
- ..Gall founded
- Romanos III
- Palaeologue Dynasty
- Constantine IX Monomachus
- Collapse of the Avars
- Greek Emperors of Nicaea
- ..Muslim attack on Sicily
- Comnene Dynasty
- Treaty of Verdun
- Christianity imposed on Russians
- ..il of Nicaea
- ..ions in Italy
- Seljuks invade Cappadocia
- Battle of Manzikert
- ..wars and Viking invasions
- Crusaders capture Jerusalem
- ..ey founded
- Third Crusade
- Otto I crowned Emperor
- Franks driven from Constantinople
- Otto III crowned Emperor
- Crusaders sack Constantinople
- ..Lorsch abbey founded
- Norman conquest of Sicily
- ..lemagne
- Battle of Hastings
- Magna Carta
- ..nagne crowned Emperor of the West

- Cappadocian rock churches
- Frescoes at Sta Sophia, Trebizond
- Aght 'amar, Armenia
- Sta Sophia, Kiev
- ..Chludov Psalter
- Hosios Lukas
- Virgin of Vladimir
- Frescoes at Boiana
- ..Church of Assumption, Nicaea
- *c.* Homilies of St John Chrysostom
- Frescoes at Milesevo
- Monastery of Lavra, Athos
- *c.* Nea Moni
- Frescoes at Nerezi
- Mistra
- Joshua Roll
- *c.* Daphni
- Ochrid *Annunciation*
- Paris Psalter
- St Clement, Ochrid
- Harbaville Triptych
- Kahrie Cami
- ..Iconoclasm
- H. Sophia, Constantinople, dome rebuilt
- Pantanassa church, Mistra
- Mosaics of Zoe and Constantine, H. Sophia
- *c.* Sermons of St Gregory of Nazianzus
- Sta Sophia, Ochrid
- Mtskhet cathedral
- Ani cathedral
- Bible of Charles the Bald
- *c.* S. Marco, Venice
- Giotto's frescoes in S. Francesco, Assisi
- ..ishop Theodulf builds Germigny des Prés
- Cefalù cathedral
- ..f Kells
- Frescoes, St Germain, Auxerre
- Martorana, Palermo
- ..Gospels
- Pala d'Oro
- Monreale cathedral
- Castelseprio frescoes
- Apse mosaic, Torcello cathedral
- ..el, Aachen
- Earls Barton church
- ..recht Psalter
- Cividale

Glossary

Abacus. Flat slab placed on top of a capital.

ad Catacumbas. Phrase originally confined to the Early Christian cemetery just outside Rome now called 'di San Sebastiano'; later extended to refer to any burial place with subterran galleries. See Catacomb.

Aediculum. Frame to a window, niche or other feature consisting of two columns supporting an entablature or pediment.

Aisle. In a church built on the plan of a basilica the aisles are the areas to either side of the nave and running parallel with it (see figures 19b, 23).

Ambo. Stand raised on two or more steps, from which the Epistle and Gospel were read; can be similar in appearance to a pulpit (see figure 25).

Ambulatory. Curved or polygonal aisle, usually leading round the sanctuary of a church.

Anastasis. Greek for 'Resurrection' (see figure 16, plate 93).

Apse. Semicircular or polygonal termination of a church, chapel or (rarely) transept. When at the east end of a church it was originally reserved for the clergy; later the altar was normally placed there (see figure 42, plate 46).

Arcade. Row of columns or pillars supporting arches, often dividing the nave of a church from the aisles; in such cases it can refer to a colonnade supporting a straight entablature (see figure 29a).
Blind arcade: a miniature arcade built into a wall for decorative purposes (see figure 66).

Architrave. Horizontal unit supported on columns; originally the lowest of the three main parts of the classical entablature (see figure 18).

Arcosolium. Ancient form of tomb often found in the catacombs. An arch was cut in the rock and the tomb hollowed out of the bottom part—a sort of natural sarcophagus (see plate 7).

Arians. Heretics named after Arius, an Alexandrian ascetic (270–336); they held that the Son of God was not eternal, but had been created by the Father from nothing. Arianism was the principal heresy of the early Church, and the first General Council at Nicaea in 325 pronounced against it, asserting the consubstantiality of the Father and the Son.

Atrium. Courtyard, often with arcades, placed in front of the main entrance to some Early Christian churches (see figure 15).

Baldachin or baldacchino. Canopy or ornamental shelter supported on columns over an altar, font, tomb or reliquary.

Baptistery. Place where a font for baptism is situated; could be either a separate building or a room within the main building of a church.

Basileus. (plural: 'basileis') Greek for 'king' or 'emperor'.

Basilica. In Early Christian architecture, a large oblong building, with a central nave and side aisles, lit by a clerestory and normally terminating in an apse.

Bema. Raised stage for the clergy; generally in the apse, or in Syria in the middle of the nave (see figure 26).

Caldarium (plural: 'caldaria') Hot room of a Roman bath.

Capital. Block of stone, usually moulded or carved, that is placed on top of a column and supports the abacus (see figures 66, 97, plate 48).

Catacomb. Underground burial-place used by the Early Christians, consisting of long tunnels lined with niches cut in the rock walls, with occasional small burial-chambers and chapels (see figure 8, plate 3).

Chlamys (plural: 'chlamydes') Short mantle or cloak, fastened by a brooch on the right shoulder and covering the whole left shoulder and arm (see plate 44).

Chrismon. Monogram of Christ (✗ or ✢), i.e. the first two letters of ΧΡΙΣΤΟΣ, reproduced by Constantine on his soldiers' standards *(labarum)*.

Circus. Roman race-track. The teams in the Circus at Constantinople, known by their colours (Reds, Greens, etc.), each had mobs of disorderly supporters and were the centre of factions and riots.

Clerestory. The part of the nave wall of a church that rises above the level of the aisles and is pierced by windows (see figure 66, plate 32).

Codex (plural: 'codices') Latin for 'book' (see figure 77).

Columbarium (plural: 'columbaria') Latin for 'dove-cote'. Tomb with small niches like pigeon-holes, to hold urns containing the ashes from cremations.

Comnenes. Dynasty of Byzantine emperors, 1071–1185. After the Macedonian dynasty had come to an end, the Comnenes came to power following a long period of disturbance; they managed to restore political stability and prolong the influence of Byzantium and Byzantine art.

Conch, Top of a semi-circular niche, *i.e.* a quarter-sphere, shaped like a conch-shell.

Corinthian. Last of the three main orders of Greek architecture. The column has a high pedestal and a capital based on acanthus foliage. It was the most popular order in Roman architecture and continued to be used in modified forms throughout the Early Christian and Byzantine periods.

Courses, coursed work. Stones or bricks laid in regular layers to make patterns of texture or colour.

Cruciform. 'Cross-shaped'. Term applied to a church of which the plan forms a cross. A church whose nave, apse and transept form a cross may be called cruciform even if the whole is contained in a rectangular outer wall (cross in square) (see figures 45, 51, 88a).

Cupola. Dome supported either on a circular wall or on four arches making a square in plan (see plate 71).

Deesis. Iconographical *schema* showing Christ between the Virgin and St. John.

Demi-column. Column set into a wall or pier for half its diameter (if for less than half, called a 'three-quarter column').

Diaconicon. In Byzantine churches, a chamber to the south of the sanctuary serving as sacristy and vestry. It was in the charge of the deacons and used for storing books, vestments and vessels needed at the altar (see figure 23).

Diaspora. The dispersion of the Jews; originally confined to parts of Egypt, Asia Minor and Asia, it eventually spread throughout the Roman Empire.

Doric. One of the orders of Greek architecture, characterized by the absence of a base to the column, thick proportions, plain capital and, in the entablature, alternating metopes and triglyphs.

Drum. (a) of a column, a cylindrical section (i.e. if the column is not monolithic).
(b) of a dome, a cylindrical wall supporting the dome and usually resting on a circle or a polygon obtained by pendentives or squinches *(q.v.)* (see plate 70).

Epiphany. Scene where the divinity of Christ is made manifest (Adoration of the Magi, Baptism, Marriage at Cana, etc.).

Epitaphios. Byzantine liturgical cloth used to cover the coffin of Christ for the Good Friday procession (see figure 93).

Exarchate. The district (remote from Constantinople) presided over by a governor owing allegiance to the Byzantine Emperor.

Exedra. Open recess; it may be rectangular or curved in plan.

Exonarthex. When there are two narthexes in a church this is the outer one, entered first by the visitor.

Extrados. Outer curve of the voussoirs of an arch, normally concentric with the intrados; also the upper surface of an arch or vault where this is visible.

Frigidarium. The part of a Roman bath where a cold plunge could be taken.

Gable roof. Roof of two slopes, triangular in section.

Henotikon. Theological formula issued in 482 under the Emperor Zeno to secure union between the Monophysites and the Orthodox.

Hetimasis. Representation of the Saviour's throne, replacing the image of Christ as king (see figure 37).

Hypogeum. Underground tomb chamber or group of chambers for private use.

Icon. Image, usually portable, of a sacred subject, person or event (see figure 56, 104, plates 111–117).

Iconography. The conveying of information by means of pictorial symbolism.

Iconoclasm. The breaking of images; the most famous outbreak of iconoclasm lasted in the Byzantine world from 726 to 843.

Iconostasis. Screen which separates the bema from the main area of an Eastern Orthodox church; it is decorated with a number of icons.

Impost. In Byzantine art, a block in the form of a truncated inverted pyramid, placed above the capital instead of an abacus.

Intrados. Under-surface of an arch or vault.

Ionic. One of the orders of Greek architecture, characterized by a low base, slender proportions, and volute capital.

Loculus (plural: 'loculi'). Commonest type of tomb in the catacombs, consisting of a horizontal rectangular niche cut in the rock wall (see figure 8, plate 7).

Macedonian. Dynasty of Byzantine emperors, 867–1057, founded by Basil I 'the Macedonian'. They gave new strength to the Empire and brought about a renaissance of the arts (see plate 55).

Mandorla. Greek for 'Almond'. An almond-shaped glory of light surrounding sacred figures such as Christ at the Ascension (see figure 21, plate 93).

Martyrion. (plural: 'Martyria') Burial-place of a saint or saints, or shrine erected on the site (see figure 30, 31).

Matroneum. Gallery over the aisle of a basilica reserved for women, when the sexes were segregated at services.

Mithraism. From Mithras. An Iranian religion practised by the Romans; it was made an Imperial cult under Commodus (180–192 AD) and was extremely popular with soldiers, with the result that Mithraic monuments are found in many frontier districts of the Roman Empire.

Monolithic. Made of a single stone.

Monophysitism. Doctrine that in the person of Christ there is only a single, and divine, nature, as distinct from the Orthodox view of the double nature of Christ—human and divine. This heresy was at its height in the mid-5th century, and the Council of Chalcedon (451) was called to anathematize it.

Moulding. Continous outline of definite shape given to the edges or surface of an architectural member (see figure 52).

Narthex. Vestibule of a church, extending along the whole of the façade (see figure 45, plate 72).

Nave. Long central area of a basilica, flanked by the aisles and lit by the clerestory (see figure 27, plates 21, 31).

Nestorians. Followers of Nestorius (died c. 451), who claimed that there were two separate persons in the incarnate Christ, one divine and the other human, in contrast to the Orthodox view of the single person of Christ who is at once both God and man.

Nika revolt. Riot that took place in 532 in Constantinople involving the different factions of the Circus *(q.v.)*; one of its results was the destruction of the Constantinian basilica of Hagia Sophia.

Nymphaeum. Roman shrine dedicated to a nymph, usually a series of niches in a wall with a fountain in front. Later extended to mean a room with an ornanamental basin or a monumental fountain.

Octagon. Figure or architectural form with eight sides (see figure 32).

Octateuch. First eight books of the Old Testament; when written on parchment, and possibly illustrated, they could be very bulky, and so were often bound separately.

Oculus. Small hole or 'eye' made in the centre of the dome of some circular Roman temples.

Orans. Latin for 'praying'. A figure in the Early Christian attitude of prayer, *i.e.* standing with arms raised (see plate 7).

Palaeologues. Dynasty of Byzantine emperors that ruled from 1261 until the fall of Constantinople in 1453; opened with Michael VIII Palaeologus and ended with Constantine XI (plates 113, 116).

Pantocrator. 'Ruler of all'. The depiction of Christ, usually bust or half-length, holding an open book of the Gospels and blessing with his right hand (see plate 73).

Parousia. The appearance of Christ in the sky on the Day of Judgment, as described in the Apocalypse.

Pax Ecclesiae. 'The peace of the Church', referring to the so called 'Edict of Milan' in 313 in which Constantine gave freedom of worship to the Christians.

Pendentive. Concave form which results when a horizontal quarter-circle is joined to two arches at right angles to each other; a 'spherical triangle'. By building pendentives in the corners of four arches forming a square, a dome or drum can be placed upon them (see figure 50).

Pilaster. Flattened out version of a column with base, fluting, capital, etc., built against a wall or pier; section of a pillar so used (see plate 27).

Pillar. Any free-standing support; can mean either a column or a support of square or oblong section.

Plinth. Low projecting course, plain or moulded, at the foot of a wall or colonnade; the base of an architectural unit or whole building.

Porphyrogenetes. 'Born in the purple'. Name given to all members of the Byzantine emperors' families who were born in a particular room of the palace which was lined with purple.

Portico. Colonnade connected by a roof to the external wall of a building. In front of a church it is a porch or narthex; around a courtyard, an atrium or cloister.

Presbyterium. The part of a church situated to the east of the choir, where the clergy sits (see figure 35).

Propylaeon. Monumental entrance to a sacred enclosure.

Proskynesis. Greek for 'Worship'. Attitude of prostration, ritual abasement before Christ or the Emperor.

Prothesis. In Byzantine churches, chamber to the north of the sanctuary where the solemn preparation of the Eucharistic gifts takes place (see figure 23).

Quatrefoil. Symmetrical shape formed by four lobes.

Reticulate. Method of wall-decoration consisting of squares set diagonally. Characteristic of the age of Augustus, revived in Carolingian buildings.

Ripidion (plural: 'ripidia') Small ceremonial fan used in Eastern Orthodox liturgy (see figure 85).

Scenae frons. Architectural background based on the scenery of the Roman theatre, which Early Christian and later artists imitated.

Squinches. Small arches built across the corners of a rectangular structure to convert the upper part to an octagon or circle. Squinches serve the same purpose as pendentives *(q.v.)* (see figure 44).

Stucco. Plaster or cement coating over stone or brick. The finest stucco was made from powdered marble.

Synaxis. In Greek churches, a public meeting for worship. Eucharistic synaxis: the Mass.

Synthronon. In the Eastern Church, bench or benches reserved for the clergy; arranged either in a semicircle in the apse or as straight rows on either side of the bema (see figures 24, 86).

Tepidarium. Room in a Roman bath intermediate in temperature between the Caldarium and the Frigidarium.

Tesserae. Small cubes of coloured marble, limestone or glass from which mosaic is made (see plate 42).

Tetrarchy. Government by four kings or emperors, ruling (over different areas) at the same time, as in the Roman Empire at the time of Diocletian, at the end of the 3rd century.

Tetrapyle. Having four gateways, *e.g.* a ceremonial arch with openings on all four sides.

Thermae. Baths, which in Roman architecture were often of great size and magnificence, and included libraries, gymnasia, etc., as well as bathing facilities.

Transept. In a cruciform church, the 'arms' of the cross; the section of the church projecting to the north and south which separates the choir or apse from the nave (see figure 19).

Trefoil. A symmetrical shape formed by three lobes.

Tufa. Common Roman building stone, volcanic in origin, of coarse porous texture. The catacombs are dug in tufa.

Tympanum. Space between the lintel of a doorway and the semicircular arch above it.

Vault. Stone roof or ceiling.
Barrel vault: continuous roof, usually semicircular in section, resting on the walls on either side.
Groined vault: roof produced by the intersection of two equal barrel-vaults. The weight of such a vault rests only on the corners.

Volumen. (plural: 'volumina') Scroll on which, before the invention of the codex, all written communications of any length had to be inscribed.

Voussoirs. Wedge-shaped blocks forming an arch.

Further Reading List

General works

Cabrol, F., Leclerq, H. et Marrou, H. *Dictionnaire d'archéologie chrétienne et de Liturgie*, 1907–53 (Librairie Letouzy et Ané)

Dalton, O. *East Christian Art, a survey of the monuments*, 1925 (Clarendon Press)

Krautheimer, R. *Early Christian and Byzantine Architecture*, 1965 (Penguin Books, Pelican History of Art)

Morey, C. R. *Early Christian Art*, 1942 (Oldbourne; Norton, New York)

Rice, D. Talbot, *The Beginnings of Christian Art*, 1957 (Hodder); 1958 (Abingdon)

Volbach, W. F. and Hirmer, M. *Early Christian Art*, 1962 (Thames and Hudson; Abrams)

The Awakening

du Bourguet, P. *Early Christian Painting*, 1965 (Weidenfeld and Nicolson)

Kirsch, J. P. *Le catacombe romane*, 1933 also in English (Società Amici delle catacombe, Rome)

Rostovtzeff, M. *Dura-Europos and its Art*, 1938 (Oxford U.P.)

Constantine

Brusin, G. e Zovatto, P. L. *Monumenti Paleocristiani di Aquileia e di Grado*, 1957 (Udine)

Crowfoot, J. W. *Early Churches in Palestine*, 1941 (Oxford U.P. for the British Academy)

Toynbee, J. M. C. and Ward Perkins, J. B. *The Shrine of St. Peter and the Vatican Excavations*, 1956 (Longmans)

Basilicas and Sanctuaries

Butler, H. C. ed. Baldwin Smith, E. *Early churches in Syria*, 1929 (Princeton)

Dyggve, E. *History of Salonitan Christianity*, 1951 (K. Paul)

Grabar, A. *Martyrium*, 1946 (Collège de France)

Lassus, J. *Sanctuaires chrétiens de Syrie*, 1944 (Paul Geuthner)

Tchalenko, G. *Villages antiques de la Syrie du Nord*, 1953 (Paris)

Ward Perkins, J. B. and Goodchild, R. G. *The Christian Antiquities of Tripolitania*, 1953 (Oxford)

Ravenna

Bovini, G. *Ravenna Mosaics*, 1956 (New York Graphic)

Deichmann, F. W. *Frühchristliche Bauten und Mosaiken von Ravenna*, 1958 (Bruno Grimm)

The Architecture of the Dome

Der Nessessian, S. *Armenia and the Byzantine Empire*, 1945 (Harvard)

Lemerle, P. *Philippes et la Macédoine orientale à l'époque chrétienne et byzantine*, 1945 (E. de Boccard)

Swift, E. H. *Hagia Sophia*, 1940 (New York)

Strzygowski, J. *Koptische Kunst*, 1904 (Vienna)

Iconography

Demus, O. *Byzantine mosaic Decoration*, 1948 (Routledge)

Grabar, A. *L'Empereur dans l'Art Byzantine*, 1936 (Paris)

Weitzmann, K. *Die Byzantinische Buchmalerei des IX und X Jahrhunderts*, 1935 (Archaeologisches Institut des Deutschen Reiches Berlin)

The West

Grabar, A. and Nordenfalk, C. *Early Medieval painting*, 1957 (Skira, Zwemmer)

Henry, F. *Irish art in the early Christian period*, 1940 (Methuen)

Hubert, J. *L'Art Préroman*, 1938 (Les éditions d'art et d'histoire)

Karl der Grosse, *Werk und Wirkung*, Exhibition 1965 (Aachen)

Koehler, W. *Die Hofschule Karls des Grossen*, 1958 (Berlin)

Sweeney, J. J. *Irish Illuminated Manuscripts*, 1965 (UNESCO Art Books, Fontana)

The Byzantine Expansion

Beckwith, J. *The Art of Constantinople*, 1961 (Phaidon; New York Graphic)

Demus, O. *The church of San Marco in Venice*, 1960 (Dumbarton Oaks)

Grabar, A. and Chadtzidakis, M. *Greece, Byzantine Church paintings and Mosaics*, 1959 (UNESCO Art Books, Studio Vista; New York Graphic)

Grabar, A. and Mijatev, K. *Bulgaria, Mediaeval Wall-Paintings*, 1962 (UNESCO Art Books, Studio Vista)

Jerphanion, J. de *Les églises rupestres de Cappadoce*, 5 vols. 1925–32 (Paris)

Kitzinger, E. *The Mosaics of Monreale*, 1960 (Palermo)

Millet, G. *Recherches sur l'iconographie de l'évangile aux XIVe, XVe et XVIe siècles*, 1916 (Fontemoing)

Rice, D. Talbot *Art of the Byzantine Era*, 1963 (Thames and Hudson)

Rice, D. Talbot and Millet, G. *Byzantine painting at Trebizond*, 1936 (Allen and Unwin)

Rice, D. Talbot and Radjcic, S. *Yugoslavia, Mediaeval Frescos*, 1955 (UNESCO Art Books, Oldbourne)

Underwood, P. A. *The Frescoes in Kariye Camii*, Dumbarton Oaks Papers, nos 9–15, 1956–61 (Harvard)

Whittemore, T. *The Mosaics of Hagia Sofia at Istanbul*, 4 vols, 1935–52 (Oxford)

Church Treasures

Alpatov, M. *Trésors de l'art Russe*, 1966 (Paris)

Ebersolt, J. *Les Arts somptuaires de Byzance*, 1923 (Editions Ernest Leroux)

Rice, T. Talbot *Russian icons*, 1963 (Spring Books)

Acknowledgements

Line drawings in this volume were based on illustrations from the publications listed below:

Grabar, Martyrium, Collège de France 30; *Lassus*, Sanctuaires de Syrie, Geuthner, Paris 4, 6, 15, 16, 17, 23, 31; *Krautheimer*, Early Christian and Byzantine Architecture, Penguin Books, London 49; *Lemerle*, Philippes et la Macedoine orientale 46; *Tchalenko*, Villages antiques de la Syrie 26, 32a; *Wulff*, Altchristliche Kunst und Byzantinische Kunst, Berlin 45, 47a, b.

Photographs were provided by the following:
Colour: Archivio Fotografico dei Civici Musei, Milan 104; F. Anderegg, University of Michigan 1, 2; C. Bevilacqua, Milan 47; Bibliothèque Nationale, Paris 63, 64, 65, 69, 99, 100; E. Boudot Lamotte, Paris 30; Bulgarski Houdoshnik, Sofia 86, 87, 88, 89; A. Duncan, Middle East Archive, London 28; Foto Ferruzi, Venice 79; Germanisches Nationalmuseum, Nuremberg 62; Giraudon, Paris 56, 57, 66, 67, 113; Green Studio, Dublin 58, 59, 60, 61; Ara Guler, Istanbul 74, 75, 93; Hessisches Landesmuseum, Darmstadt 68; Hirmer Verlag, Munich 45, 98, 117; Michael Holford, London 14, 105; D. Hughes-Gilbey, London 71, 72; Geraldine Kenway, Athens 70, 73, 94, 95; A. F. Kersting, London 26, 27, 84; F. A. Mella, Milan 18, 19, 41, 102; S. Mileusnic, Belgrade 85; Ann Munchow, Aachen 53; Österreichische Nationalbibliothek, Vienna 97; Pierpont Morgan Library, New York 106; Josephine Powell, Rome 90, 91, 92, 96; Rapho, Paris 51, 52, 54; Réunion des Musées Nationaux, Versailles 104; Scala, Florence 15, 16, 17, 22, 23, 24, 25, 29, 31, 32, 33, 34, 35, 36, 37, 38, 39, 40, 42, 43, 44, 48, 49, 50, 55, 77, 78, 80, 107, 115; E. Sellerio, Palermo 81, 82, 83; Society for Cultural Relations with U.S.S.R., London 114; David Talbot Rice, Edinburgh 76; Thames and Hudson, London 111; Tretyakov Gallery, Moscow 112; Vasari, Rome 6, 20, 21; Victoria and Albert Museum, London 116; John Webb, London 108, 109, 110; Roger Wood, London 46; J. P. Ziolo/André Held, Paris 3, 4, 5, 7, 8, 9, 10, 11, 12, 13.

Black and white: A. C. L. Brussels 64; Alinari, Florence 2, 27, 36, 82, 84, 97a; Alinari/Anderson, Florence 14, 37, 38, 40a, 41e, 59; Bibliothèque Nationale, Paris 53, 57; Bildarchiv Foto Marburg 20, 35, 66, 73a, 88, 90, 92; Osvaldo Bohm Fotografico, Venice 24, 44, 96; Boudot-Lamotte, Paris 34, 49b, 74; British School, Rome 25; Bulgarski Houdoshnik, Sofia 87; Collège des Hautes Etudes, Paris 61; Cleveland Museum of Art, Ohio 98; Duke University Library, North Carolina 94; John Freeman, London 10a; German Archeological Institute, Rome 41a, 41b, 41d; Giraudon, Paris 95; Mladen Grcevic, Zagreb 85a, 85b, 85c, 86; Green Studio, Dublin 71, 72; Ara Guler, Istanbul 50, 81a, 89; Studio Haig, Amman 18; Paul Hamlyn Archive 22, 52, 56, 60, 83, 104; Atelier Niko Haus, Trier 76; Hirmer Verlag, Munich 11, 12, 13, 21, 39, 40b, 42, 78; D. Hughes-Gilbey, London 79a; Geraldine Kenway, Athens 58, 79b, 91, 93; A. F. Kersting, London 43; Kungliga Biblioteket, Stockholm 77; Professor Jean Lassus, Paris 1, 5, 7, 19a, 29a, 29b, 32b; Louvre Photographic Service, Paris 101; Metropolitan Museum of Art, New York 100; Musée d'Art et Histoire, Fribourg 65; National Buildings Record, London 70; Pierpont Morgan Library, New York 102; Princeton University Library 103; Princeton University, Department of Art and Archeology 33; Pontificia Commissione di Archeologia Sacra, Vatican City 8; Josephine Powell, Rome 48, 81b, 97b; Jean Roubier, Paris 62; Guido Sansoni, Rome 55; Edwin Smith, Saffron Walden 75; Stadtarchiv, Aachen 73c; E. Stawski 28; Fotokronika Tass, Moscow 51; Turkish Tourist Office, London 81c; Vatican Library, Vatican City 54; Worcester Art Museum, Massachusetts 99; John Webb, London 9; Joseph Ziolo – André Held, Paris 10b; Zodiaque Press, St. Leger Vauban 67, 68, 69a, 69b, 69c; *Illustration facing page 6, Max Hirmer*.

The Early Christian and Byzantine World

■ Maximum extent of Byzantine World
▲ Places with domed monuments of Byzantine influence

Iona
Lindisfarne
NORTHUMBERLAND
Londonderry
Bewcastle
Kells
IRELAND
Durrow
Ardagh
Earls Barton

FRIESLAND

R. Rhine

Hersfeld
Fulda
Aachen
Lorsch
Wingles
Echternach Trier

R. Danube

Paris Jouarre
Luxeuil
Germigny des Prés
St Gall
Auxerre
Tours
Cividale
Aquileia Grado
Poitiers
Torcello ISTRIA
Como Venice
Castelseprio Monza
Pavia Milan R. Po
Grenoble
Bobbio Ravenna
Conques
Classis
Riez
Albenga
ADRIATIC SEA
Toulouse
Fréjus
Marseille
Rome
Oviedo
Pompeii
Pyrenees

Tarrasa

Monreale Cefalù
Palermo
Piazza Arme

SICILY

Hippo Regius
Sousse
Cherchel Tipasa
Djemila
Timgad
Tebessa